# Navigating the Metaverse:

## A Developer's Guide to the Next Internet Frontier.

**ISHAN ROY**

## Copyright Page

Copyright © 2024 All rights reserved.

No part of this publication may be reproduced, distributed, or transmitted in any form or by any means, including photocopying, recording, or other electronic or mechanical methods, without the prior written permission of the publisher, except in the case of brief quotations embodied in critical reviews and certain other noncommercial uses permitted by copyright law.

**Disclaimer:**

The information in this book is provided "as is" without warranty of any kind, either express or implied, including but not limited to the warranties of merchantability, fitness for a particular purpose, or non-infringement. The author and publisher shall not be liable for any damages arising from the use of this book.

# TABLE OF CONTENT

| | |
|---|---|
| **Introduction** | 5 |
| **Overview of Metaverse Creation** | 5 |
| **Chapter One** | 14 |
| **Foundations of Development of Metaverses** | 14 |
| ➢ Foundational Technologies for Metaverse Creation: VR, AR, Blockchain, AI, IoT | 25 |
| ➢ Comprehending Digital Realities and Virtual Worlds | 33 |
| **Chapter Two** | 43 |
| **Technical Framework for the Development of the Metaverse** | 43 |
| ➢ Hardware Requirements: VR Headsets, AR Glasses, and More | 52 |
| ➢ Platforms and Software for Metaverse Development | 60 |
| ➢ Cloud Infrastructure and Networking | 70 |
| Chapter Three | 79 |
| Constructing Virtual Environments | 79 |
| ➢ 3D Modeling and Graphics | 88 |
| ➢ Crafting Immersive Metaverse Experiences | 98 |
| ➢ Designing User Experience (UX) and User Interface (UI) | 107 |
| **Chapter Four** | 117 |
| **Building Applications for the Metaverse** | 117 |
| ➢ Development of VR and AR Applications | 127 |
| ➢ Blockchain and NFT Integration in the Metaverse | 137 |

- ➢ Using Machine Learning and AI in the Metaverse 147

## Chapter Five — 156
## The Metaverse Economy — 156
- ➢ Digital Assets and Virtual Economies — 164
- ➢ Case Studies of Profitable Metaverse Efforts — 171

## Chapter Six — 175
## Social and Ethical Factors in the Development of the Metaverse — 175
- ➢ Security and Privacy Issues — 183
- ➢ Ethical Implications of Metaverse Interaction — 188

## Chapter Seven — 193
## Case Studies and Practical Illustrations in the Development of the Metaverse — 193
- ➢ Examining Current Metaverse Platforms — 203
- ➢ Metaverse Development Success Stories and Failures to Learn from — 215
- ➢ Interviews with Metaverse Development Industry Leaders — 226

## Chapter Eight — 234
## Upcoming Developments and Trends in the Metaverse — 234
- ➢ New Developments and Technologies in the Metaverse — 243
- ➢ Future Forecasts for the Metaverse — 252
- ➢ Preparing for What's Next in the Metaverse — 260

## Conclusion — 269

# Introduction

## Overview of Metaverse Creation

Science fiction has quickly given way to one of the most fascinating technological frontiers: the Metaverse. The Metaverse, a digital environment that combines virtual and augmented reality (AR/VR) with physical reality, heralds a new era of immersive, networked experiences. This brief introduction delves into the fundamental components, importance, and game-changing possibilities of Metaverse development.

- **Define the Metaverse**

The fusion of physically permanent virtual places with virtually augmented physical reality has produced the Metaverse, a communal virtual shared space. It encompasses all virtual environments, augmented reality, and the internet, where people can communicate with one another and a computer-generated environment. In this notion, individuals can participate in a wide range of activities from gaming and socialising to conducting business and receiving education inside a massive digital ecosystem.

- **Background History and Development**

Neal Stephenson first used the word "Metaverse" in his science fiction book Snow Crash from 1992, which envisioned a virtual reality-based internet replacement. Technology has advanced over the last few decades, bringing this vision closer to reality. The development of the Metaverse has been characterised by important technological turning points, ranging from the first virtual worlds like Second Life to the current VR platforms like Oculus and AR games like Pokémon GO.

- **Fundamental Technologies Powered by the Metaverse**

The Metaverse's development is supported by several important technologies:

**1. Augmented Reality (AR) and Virtual Reality (VR):** While AR superimposes digital data on the real world, VR creates a virtual environment that allows for truly immersive experiences. They serve as the framework for the Metaverse, providing users with a smooth transition between virtual and real-world worlds.

**2. Blockchain:** Blockchain technology makes ownership and transactions in the Metaverse safe and transparent. It makes it possible to create decentralised digital assets, including non-fungible tokens (NFTs), which can be used to signify ownership of digital goods like artwork and other things.

**3. Artificial Intelligence (AI):** AI powers dynamic virtual environments, intelligent avatars, and tailored user experiences, all of which improve the Metaverse. By analysing user behaviour, machine learning algorithms generate digital landscapes that are both dynamic and adaptable.

**4. Internet of Things (IoT):** IoT enables physical objects to communicate with one another inside the Metaverse by connecting them to the internet. User experiences are improved by this integration, which makes it easier for users to engage seamlessly between the virtual and real worlds.

**5. Cloud Computing:** To manage and render intricate virtual worlds, the Metaverse needs a massive amount of processing power. Scalability and performance are guaranteed by the infrastructure that cloud computing offers to meet these expectations.

- **The Significance and Possible Effect on Diverse Industries**

The Metaverse has the potential to revolutionise many different fields:

**1. Entertainment and Gaming:** The Metaverse has enormous potential benefits for the entertainment sector. The boundaries between reality and fantasy can be blurred via virtual concerts, immersive gaming, and interactive storytelling, which can provide previously unheard-of experiences.

**2. Education and Training:** By offering immersive learning settings, the Metaverse can completely transform the field of education. To meet a range of learning demands, virtual classrooms, interactive simulations, and remote training can improve accessibility and participation.

**3. Healthcare:** Virtual consultations, medical education, and mental health therapy can all be facilitated by the Metaverse. Training results and patient care can be enhanced by the realistic simulations of medical procedures that VR and AR can provide.

**4. Business and Commerce:** New avenues for virtual meetings, remote work, and e-commerce are made possible by the Metaverse. To increase efficiency and engage customers, businesses can set up virtual stores, hold virtual events, and cooperate in immersive spaces.

**5. Social Interaction:** Within the Metaverse, social media platforms have the potential to develop into completely immersive social places. Deeper connections can be cultivated by users' ability to communicate with friends, participate in virtual events, and explore online communities.

- **Difficulties and Moral Issues**

The Metaverse faces a number of problems in addition to its potential for great breakthroughs.

**1. Privacy and Security:** Privacy and security issues are brought up by the combination of virtual identities and personal data. Sustaining confidence in the Metaverse depends on safeguarding user data and averting online attacks.

**2. Digital Divide:** Having access to the Metaverse necessitates high-tech gear and internet access, which could widen the digital divide. It is crucial to guarantee fair access in order to stop marginalisation.

**3. Governance and Regulation:** The decentralised structure of the Metaverse presents difficulties for governance and regulation. Concerns like digital ownership and content moderation will require the establishment of legal frameworks and ethical standards.

**4. Mental Health:** Extended use of virtual environments may have negative effects on one's mental state. Preventing potential detrimental effects on wellbeing requires striking a balance between digital and physical connections.

- **Prospective Patterns and Advancements**

The Metaverse is still in its early phases, and new developments will continue to shape it in the future:

**1. Interoperability:** The foundation for a smooth user experience across various Metaverse platforms will be the standards and protocols developed for interoperability. Users will be able to move between virtual worlds with ease if common frameworks are established.

**2. Technological Developments:** More widespread usage will be fueled by the creation of more accessible and reasonably priced VR/AR gear. Users will have better experiences because of innovations like lighter headsets, haptic feedback, and better motion tracking.

**3. AI and Personalisation:** AI will be essential to adjusting Metaverse experiences to each individual. Smart algorithms will build settings that are dynamic and adaptive, based on the tastes and actions of each individual.

**4. Expansion of Virtual Economies:** As virtual economies expand, new economic opportunities and business models will arise. The Metaverse economy will include digital assets, virtual real estate, and decentralised finance (DeFi).

The emergence of the metaverse signifies a paradigm shift in the way we engage with both virtual and real-world environments. Through the use of cutting-edge technologies, the Metaverse presents countless opportunities for innovation in a wide range of industries. Building a diverse, safe, and dynamic digital environment will depend heavily on how we handle the difficulties and moral issues that arise as we traverse this new territory. The goal of this book is to give readers a thorough understanding of the Metaverse and the skills they need to grow within it and contribute to its future development.

This brief introduction lays the groundwork for a more thorough examination of the Metaverse's development and gives readers a comprehensive grasp of its importance, possibilities, and the technology guiding its advancement.

# Chapter One

# Foundations of Development of Metaverses

The word "metaverse," which was hitherto exclusive to science fiction, is increasingly being used to describe our digital environment. The Metaverse, which combines physically persistent virtual environments with virtually augmented physical reality, has the potential to completely transform how we connect, work, and play. This in-depth examination of the foundations of Metaverse development will cover its underlying technologies, guiding concepts, and essential elements that give life to this virtual world.

- **Determining the Metaverse's Scope**

The internet and digitally augmented physical reality came together to form the Metaverse, which is a collective virtual shared world. This area is everlasting, offering consistent and flawless user experiences on a range of platforms and gadgets. It combines elements of virtual reality (VR), augmented reality (AR), and the internet to enable real-time user interaction with a computer-generated environment and other users.

- **Fundamental Technologies Powered by the Metaverse**

The following fundamental technologies are necessary for the Metaverse's development:

**1. Virtual Reality (VR) and Augmented Reality (AR)**

- Virtual Reality (VR): VR immerses users in a computer-generated world, offering a completely immersive digital experience. Users can explore and interact with 3D worlds as if they were physically present by donning VR goggles.

- Augmented Reality (AR): AR improves a user's perception and engagement with their surroundings by superimposing digital information over the actual world. AR apps combine the digital and physical worlds; they can be accessed through gadgets like smartphones and AR glasses.

## 2. Blockchain Technology

Blockchain is essential to creating confidence in the Metaverse and guaranteeing safe transactions. It makes it possible to develop decentralised apps (dApps) and digital assets like non-fungible tokens (NFTs), which can stand in for ownership of real estate, virtual products, and other things.

## 3. Artificial Intelligence (AI)

AI underpins a lot of the Metaverse, including personalised and dynamic world-building, intelligent avatars, and non-player characters (NPCs). In order to build responsive, adaptable environments that improve user experiences, machine learning algorithms examine user behaviour.

## 4. Internet of Things (IoT)

IoT allows physical objects to communicate with each other inside the Metaverse by connecting them to the internet. The ability to seamlessly incorporate physical objects and activities into digital spaces is made possible by this link, which improves the functionality and realism of virtual environments.

## 5. Cloud Computing

Cloud computing provides the enormous processing capacity needed to sustain the Metaverse. In order to manage the intricate procedures involved in rendering, data storage, and real-time interactions, cloud services provide scalable and adaptable resources.

- **Creating the Metaverse: Essential Elements**

Several essential elements must come together to create a useful and captivating metaverse:

**1.3D Modelling and Graphics** - Realistic virtual environments cannot be created without excellent 3D modelling. The resources required to create and depict intricate and engrossing worlds are provided by graphics engines like Unity and Unreal Engine.

**2. Designing User Experience (UX) and User Interface (UI)** - For user engagement, a smooth UX and an easy-to-use UI are essential. In order to minimise friction and improve the user experience overall, designers must make sure that interactions inside the Metaverse are natural and easy to use.

**3. Networking and Connectivity** - To enable in-the-moment user interactions, the Metaverse needs a strong networking infrastructure. A seamless and responsive virtual experience depends on having fast internet, minimal latency, and effective data transfer.

**4. Interoperability** - Different virtual worlds and platforms need to be able to communicate with one another in order for the Metaverse to be fully integrated.

In order to allow users to transition between different Metaverse contexts without losing their digital identity or assets, standards and protocols are being established.

- **Building Applications for the Metaverse**

Application development for the Metaverse entails a few crucial steps:

**1. Planning and Conceptualization** - It's critical to have a clear understanding of the application's goal, target market, and essential features before development ever starts. Planning ahead thoroughly guarantees that the development process is effective and in line with the desired user experience.

**2. Selecting the Proper Development Platform** - Developers must decide the platforms and tools to use in accordance with the specifications of the application. While blockchain platforms like Ethereum give the basis for developing decentralised applications, platforms like Unity and Unreal Engine offer strong frameworks for developing VR and AR applications.

**3. Creating Immersive Experiences** - A Metaverse application's capacity to deliver captivating and immersive experiences is what determines its level of success. This entails creating responsive and adaptable worlds through the use of AI, realistic physics, and interactive environment design.

**4. Testing and Optimisation** - To find and fix any problems that can affect the user experience, thorough testing is necessary. Performance optimisation makes sure that the programme functions properly on many devices and in various network scenarios.

**5. Privacy and Security** - In the Metaverse, security is crucial because of the possibility of data breaches and cyberattacks. Strong security measures must be put in place by developers to safeguard user information and guarantee the integrity of the virtual environment.

Additionally important are privacy concerns, which necessitate adherence to pertinent laws and industry best practices.

- **Difficulties and Points to Take**

Creating the Metaverse involves a number of difficulties:

**1. Technical Complexity** - A large amount of technical know-how and funding are needed to integrate different technologies, including blockchain, VR, AR, and AI. It is a difficult undertaking to make sure that these components interact seamlessly.

**2. Scalability** - As the Metaverse expands, it is essential to make sure that the infrastructure can grow to support more users and intricate interactions. Effective resource management and cutting-edge networking solutions are needed for this.

**3. User Adoption** - The perceived value of the experiences provided, hardware affordability, and user-friendliness are the key factors in promoting the broad adoption of Metaverse apps. Building a strong user base requires removing the early obstacles to entrance.

**4. Legal and Ethical Concerns** - Important moral and legal concerns are brought up by the Metaverse, such as those involving digital identity, data ownership, and user consent. Carefully navigating these obstacles is necessary for developers to provide a secure and welcoming virtual environment.

- **The Metaverse's Development in the Future**

The Metaverse is still in its infancy, and it will continue to evolve as long as advances are made. Potential future developments could be:

**1. Enhanced Interactivity** - Users will be able to feel and manipulate virtual items in the Metaverse thanks to developments in haptic technology and motion tracking, which will make interactions more realistic and captivating.

**2. Introduced Virtual Markets** - The expansion of virtual economies and digital assets will open up new doors for innovation and entrepreneurship. A few such business initiatives are virtual services, digital fashion, and virtual real estate.

**3. Broader Accessibility** - Lowering hardware prices, enhancing connection, and developing inclusive designs that meet a range of user needs will be the main goals of efforts to make the Metaverse more accessible.

**4. Integration with Physical Reality** - Real-world data and activities will be more seamlessly integrated into the Metaverse, further blurring the boundaries between the virtual and physical worlds. This will improve the virtual experiences' relevancy and reality.

The technology, ideas, and elements that come together to form immersive and dynamic virtual worlds are all part of the Metaverse development foundations. Developers may help the Metaverse expand and change by being aware of these fundamental components, which will open up new avenues for creativity and interaction. The Metaverse holds the potential to revolutionise our way of living, working, and interacting in the virtual era as we investigate and expand this new frontier in technology.

## ➢ Foundational Technologies for Metaverse Creation: VR, AR, Blockchain, AI, IoT

Numerous state-of-the-art technologies support the Metaverse, a smooth fusion of the real and virtual worlds. The development of the permanent, interactive, and immersive virtual worlds that characterise the Metaverse depends heavily on these fundamental technologies. The main technologies that are propelling the development of the Metaverse will be discussed in this section: blockchain, augmented reality, virtual reality, artificial intelligence, and the Internet of Things (IoT).

- **Virtual Reality (VR):**

Virtual Reality (VR) is one of the Metaverse's core technologies. Users are thoroughly submerged in a computer-generated environment as a result of this fully immersive digital experience. Virtual reality seeks to build imaginary worlds that are only constrained by the user's imagination or to reproduce real-world experiences. VR adds the following to the Metaverse:

**1. Immersion:** Virtual reality gives users a sensation of presence, giving them the impression that they are in a new environment. This is made possible by virtual reality (VR) headsets, which track head motions and project 3D images to provide a 360-degree picture of the virtual world.

**2. Interaction:** With the help of motion sensors and hand controllers, users of advanced VR systems can interact naturally and intuitively with the virtual world. For tasks like virtual meetings, training simulations, and gaming, this contact is essential.

**3. Applications:** Virtual reality (VR) can be utilised to create virtual workplaces, entertainment centres, learning environments, and hubs for social interaction within the Metaverse. Regardless of where they are physically located, these places provide new means for people to interact and work together.

- **Virtual and Augmented Reality**

By superimposing digital data on top of the real environment, **Augmented Reality (AR)** improves it. AR creates a mixed reality experience by fusing virtual and real-world aspects, unlike VR, which builds an entirely simulated world. In the Metaverse, augmented reality is important in the following ways:

**1. Overlay Information:** AR may project contextual data—like product specifications, navigational instructions, or user interfaces—directly onto real-world items. The user's interaction with their surroundings is improved as a result.

**2. Enhanced Experiences:** Augmented reality (AR) can improve in-person experiences by fusing digital and physical aspects. For instance, augmented reality (AR) can be utilised in retail to let buyers see things in their homes, in education to offer interactive course materials, and in the medical field to show patients' medical data while they are having surgery.

**3. Devices:** AR may be accessed on a range of gadgets, such as tablets, smartphones, and AR glasses. These gadgets eliminate the need for specialised VR gear by allowing users to experience the Metaverse in their regular surroundings.

- **Blockchain Technology**

A decentralised digital ledger called **Blockchain** guarantees data security, immutability, and transparency. It is an essential piece of technology for the Metaverse, especially when it comes to proving ownership and trust in virtual environments. This is how blockchain advances the growth of the Metaverse:

1. **Decentralisation:** Within the Metaverse, decentralised apps (dApps) and services can be developed thanks to blockchain technology. Fairness and security are enhanced by this decentralisation, which makes sure that no one entity has power over the entire virtual environment.

2. **Digital Ownership**: Non-fungible tokens (NFTs), or distinct digital assets, can be created and managed on a blockchain. NFTs give consumers a safe way to purchase, sell, and exchange products by serving as a means of identifying ownership of virtual goods, real estate, artwork, and other assets within the Metaverse.

**3. Smart Contracts:** Smart contracts built on blockchain technology automate deals and uphold agreements without the need for middlemen. In the Metaverse, these contracts are meant to enable safe and open transactions, including renting virtual places or gaining access to premium content.

- **Artificial Intelligence (AI)**

The Metaverse is improved by Artificial Intelligence (AI), which offers individualised, intelligent, and responsive experiences. AI technologies, such as computer vision, natural language processing, and machine learning, are important to the development of the metaverse in a number of ways.

**1. Intelligent Avatars:** AI-enabled avatars are capable of lifelike user interaction. The Metaverse is made more dynamic and engaging by these avatars' ability to comprehend and respond to normal language, identify emotions, and modify their behaviour in response to user interactions.

**2. Dynamic Environments:** Artificial intelligence algorithms are capable of creating and overseeing dynamic virtual environments that adapt and change in response to user choices and activities. Users will have a more engaging and customised experience as a result.

**3. Content Creation:** Artificial intelligence (AI) tools help with content creation and Metaverse optimisation. AI saves time and effort in content production, freeing developers to concentrate on innovation. It can create realistic 3D models and intricate simulations.

- **Internet of Things (IoT)**

The Internet of Things (IoT) enables the collection and sharing of data by connecting physical objects to the internet. IoT increases the realism and usefulness of virtual environments by bridging the gap between the real and digital worlds in the context of the Metaverse:

**1. Real-Time Data Integration:** Location data, user biometrics, and ambient variables are just a few examples of the real-time data that IoT devices may supply. With the utilisation of this data, virtual experiences could be made more precise and responsive.

**2. Improved Interactions:** Internet of Things allows physical devices to communicate with digital worlds. For instance, activities in the actual world can initiate events in virtual environments, allowing for a smooth blending of worlds. Smart home appliances can also be managed from within the Metaverse.

**3. Wearables and Sensors:** Smart glasses and fitness trackers are examples of wearable Internet of Things (IoT) technologies that can improve user interactions with the Metaverse. By offering more inputs and feedback, these gadgets enhance the immersive experience as a whole.

The creation of the Metaverse is an intricate and varied project that depends on the fusion of numerous cutting-edge technology. Blockchain guarantees safe transactions and ownership, while Virtual Reality (VR) and Augmented Reality (AR) produce immersive and interactive environments. The Internet of Things (IoT) connects the physical and digital realms, while artificial intelligence (AI) improves the intelligence and personalisation of virtual encounters. These technologies, when combined, provide the Metaverse's framework, allowing for the construction of an ever-changing, networked digital world with countless opportunities for creativity and interaction. The Metaverse will definitely change how we interact, work, and live in the digital age as we investigate and develop these technologies more.

## ➢ Comprehending Digital Realities and Virtual Worlds

The creation of the Metaverse, a vast digital cosmos that combines aspects of the actual and virtual worlds, is largely dependent on the ideas of virtual worlds and digital realities. Immersion experiences ranging from fully simulated universes to augmented layers of information over the real world are provided by these virtual environments. Comprehending these ideas is essential to understanding how the Metaverse functions and how it has the potential to transform our relationships with technology and one another.

- **What Is A Virtual Environment?**

Computer-generated settings known as Virtual Worlds allow users to engage in real-time interaction with the environment and one another. These settings can be entirely virtual or include features from the actual world. The capacity of virtual worlds to recreate intricate situations and offer participatory experiences is what sets them apart. Virtual worlds' salient characteristics include:

**1. Immersion:** The goal of virtual worlds is to give people the impression that they are actually there in the virtual environment. Advanced visuals, 3D modelling, and often virtual reality (VR) technology are used to create this immersion.

**2. Interactivity:** Users can communicate with one other and their surroundings in virtual environments. This involvement can take the form of playing games, interacting with others, navigating virtual environments, or carrying out business operations.

**3. Persistence:** A lot of virtual worlds run constantly, so even when people aren't actively participating, the environment continues to change and exist. This durability makes it possible for conversations and advancements to continue in the virtual environment.

**4. Customisation**: Avatars, settings, and experiences can be customised by users in virtual worlds. Users are better engaged and are able to forge their own identities online because of this personalisation.

- **Virtual World Types**

**1. Online games with many players, or MMOs):** These are expansive virtual environments where users converse with one another in a common space. Multiplayer online games (MMOs) that provide social connections and immersive, interactive experiences include World of Warcraft and Second Life.

**2. Social Virtual Worlds:** Social interactions and community development are the main focus of sites like AltspaceVR and Second Life. Users can attend events, build and explore virtual locations, and engage in more casual and laid-back social interactions.

**3. Simulation Environments:** These are virtual environments created for specialised uses, such instruction, training, or study. Virtual labs for scientific research and flight simulators used for pilot instruction are two examples.

- **Can You Explain Digital Realities?**

An even wider variety of experiences that combine digital and physical components are referred to as Digital Realities. They consist of mixed reality (MR) and augmented reality (AR), which combine digital data to expand and improve our perspective of the physical world.

**1. Augmented Reality (AR):** AR superimposes digital data on the actual environment. You can experience this with gadgets like AR glasses, tablets, and smartphones. Applications for augmented reality (AR) can present interactive components, visual improvements, and contextual data to enhance how users interact with their environment.

**2. Mixed Reality (MR):** By fusing aspects of AR and VR, MR improves the interoperability of interactions between real-world and virtual environments. Users of MR technologies can simultaneously interact with virtual and real-world items. Examples of MR technology devices are the HoloLens from Microsoft.

- **Essential Ideas in Digital Realities and Virtual Worlds**

**1. Digital Avatars:** In virtual worlds, avatars are digital depictions of users. They may interact with the environment and other avatars, and they can be customised to match the user's preferences. In virtual environments, avatars are essential for facilitating interpersonal communication and self-expression.

**2. Virtual Economies:** A lot of virtual worlds have their own marketplaces where people may exchange virtual products and services for cash. These economies are frequently supported by blockchain technology and digital currencies, which enable safe and open transactions.

**3. Spatial Computing:** The technology that makes it possible for digital interactions to take place in three-dimensional spaces is known as spatial computing. In order to develop immersive worlds where users can interact with spatial data and objects, this includes using VR and AR.

**4. User-Generated Content:** Users can produce and distribute their own virtual experiences, environments, and objects in a lot of virtual worlds. The diversity and richness of the virtual environment are improved by this user-generated content.

- **Use Cases and Applications**

**1. Entertainment and Gaming:** From video games to virtual concerts, virtual worlds and digital realities provide immersive entertainment experiences. Users can connect with digital information and other participants in novel ways in these environments.

**2. Education and Training:** Simulations and interactive learning opportunities are provided by virtual environments. Virtual classrooms, career-specific training simulations, and interactive instructional games are a few examples.

**3. Healthcare:** Digital realities and virtual worlds are utilised in healthcare for patient care, therapy, and medical education. Medical personnel can practise operations with the aid of virtual simulations, and AR applications can help with diagnosis and surgeries.

**4. Social Interaction:** Users can engage and connect with others in novel and interesting ways through social virtual worlds and augmented reality applications. Social networking in immersive virtual environments, cooperative initiatives, and virtual get-togethers are made possible by these technologies.

- **Difficulties and Points to Take**

**1. Technical Complexity:** There are several technical obstacles in the creation and upkeep of virtual worlds and digital realities. As part of this, real-time performance, interactivity, and graphics must all be seamlessly integrated.

**2. Human Experience**: A thorough grasp of human behaviour and preferences is necessary to design captivating and easy-to-use experiences in virtual and digital environments. For adoption to be widely diffused, accessibility and usability must be guaranteed.

**3. Privacy and Security:** Safeguarding user information and facilitating safe communications in virtual settings are top priorities. It is imperative for developers to incorporate strong security protocols in order to protect user data and avert online dangers.

**4. Ethical and Social Implications:** As digital realities and virtual worlds proliferate, significant ethical and social issues are brought to light. These include concerns about virtual property rights, digital identity, and the possible effects on social behaviour and mental health.

Comprehending virtual worlds and digital realities is essential to fully appreciating the Metaverse's potential. These ideas offer the foundation for developing interactive, immersive experiences that combine the real and virtual worlds. Virtual worlds and digital realities will become more and more prevalent as technology develops, influencing how people communicate, work, and live in a digitally connected world. We may better understand the Metaverse's revolutionary potential and how it can reshape our digital experiences by delving into these principles.

# Chapter Two

# Technical Framework for the Development of the Metaverse

The Metaverse unites the virtual and physical worlds into a single, holistic experience, signalling a revolutionary step forward in digital engagement. An extensive and dynamic environment like this requires a strong technical infrastructure. This infrastructure consists of a number of parts, including networking, data management systems, hardware, and software. We'll examine the vital components of the technological framework required to create and maintain the Metaverse in this investigation.

**1. System specifications**

For the Metaverse to provide immersive experiences, cutting-edge hardware is essential. The primary hardware elements consist of:

**Virtual Reality (VR) Headsets:** Creating immersive experiences requires the use of VR headsets. High-resolution screens, accurate motion tracking, and spatial audio are features offered by devices like as the Oculus Rift, HTC Vive, and PlayStation VR. For these headsets to produce a realistic virtual experience, they need strong processing power and sensors.

**Augmented Reality (AR) Devices:** AR gadgets superimpose digital data on the physical world. Examples of AR devices are Microsoft HoloLens and Magic Leap. These gadgets use computers, cameras, and sensors to combine digital material with the real world, giving users interactive and contextual experiences.

**High-Performance Computers:** Robust computing resources are needed to build and sustain the Metaverse. Complex 3D environments and real-time interactions require powerful GPUs, lots of RAM, and quick processors, which can only be achieved with high-performance PCs or servers.

**Networking Equipment:** The Metaverse depends on a dependable, fast networking infrastructure. This comprises servers, switches, and routers that control data flow, guarantee minimal latency, and facilitate smooth user and virtual environment connectivity.

## 2. Development Tools and Software Platforms

A variety of software platforms and development tools that facilitate the creation, administration, and optimisation of virtual environments are used in the development of the Metaverse. These include:

**Game Engines:** The basis for creating fully immersive 3D environments is game engines like Unity and Unreal Engine. These engines give programmers the means to create, render, and programme virtual environments. They facilitate features like interactive components, physics simulation, and real-time graphics.

**3D Modelling and Animation Software:** 3D models for the Metaverse are created and animated using programmes like Blender, Maya, and 3ds Max. The intricate creation of items, locations, and avatars is made possible by these software programmes, guaranteeing excellent visual experiences.

**Augmented Reality SDKs:** To create AR applications, Software Development Kits (SDKs) like ARKit (for iOS) and ARCore (for Android) are necessary. These SDKs offer frameworks and instruments, such as motion tracking, gesture recognition, and spatial mapping, for fusing digital material with the real world.

**Blockchain Platforms:** Digital assets and transactions, as well as many other features of the Metaverse, are supported by blockchain technology. Ensuring safe and transparent interactions, platforms such as Ethereum and Binance Smart Chain make it easier to create decentralised apps (dApps) and handle non-fungible tokens (NFTs).

## 3. Connectivity and Networking

High-performance networking infrastructure is required by the Metaverse to facilitate large-scale virtual environments and real-time interactions:

**Low Latency and High Bandwidth:** Networks must offer low latency and high bandwidth in order to facilitate a flawless Metaverse experience. This guarantees that users, even in intricate or highly inhabited virtual environments, encounter minimal latency and seamless interactions.

**Content Delivery Networks (CDNs):** In order to lower latency and increase access speeds, CDNs distribute content among several servers. They are essential for effectively providing people all across the world with content like textures, models, and movies.

**Edge Computing:** By processing data closer to the user, edge computing lowers latency and boosts efficiency. This is especially crucial for real-time response applications, such interactive virtual reality experiences and live virtual events.

## 4. Storage and Data Management

Because of the massive volumes of data generated by the Metaverse, effective data management and storage solutions are required:

**Cloud processing:** Scalable processing and storage resources are offered by cloud platforms such as Microsoft Azure, Google Cloud, and Amazon Web Services (AWS). The Metaverse's resource-intensive and dynamic needs, such as data processing, backup, and storage, are met via cloud services.

**Databases:** User information, virtual assets, and application states must all be managed via databases. Depending on the type and volume of data, relational databases (like MySQL, PostgreSQL) and NoSQL databases (like MongoDB, Cassandra) are used.

**Data Security and Privacy:** In the Metaverse, safeguarding user data and maintaining privacy are vital concerns. To protect sensitive data and stop unwanted access, secure data storage techniques, access controls, and encryption are used.

## 5. Designing the User Interface and Experience

In order to make interactions in the Metaverse easy to use and entertaining, user interface (UI) and user experience (UX) design are essential:

**User Interaction Models:** Developing logical controls and gestures is a necessary step in designing efficient VR and AR interaction models. Creating intuitive means for users to interact, move around, and converse in the virtual environment is part of this.

**Accessibility and Usability:** Taking into account a range of characteristics, including physical infirmities, visual impairments, and differing technical skill, is necessary to guarantee that the Metaverse is usable by a varied audience. All users will find a more user-friendly experience thanks to inclusive design techniques.

**Immersive Experience Design:** Realistic graphics, responsive interactions, spatial audio, and other details must all be carefully considered when creating immersive experiences. This entails creating settings that give a sense of presence and respond dynamically to human input.

## 6. Optimisation of Scalability and Performance

Scalability and performance optimisation become more crucial as the Metaverse develops:

**Load Balancing:** To guarantee dependable performance and avoid overload, load balancing divides user requests and computing workloads among several servers. Maintaining stability and responsiveness in situations with heavy traffic requires doing this.

**Performance Monitoring and Tuning:** To locate and remove bottlenecks, systems must be regularly monitored and tuned. Code optimisation, better resource management, and hardware upgrades when required to keep up with demand are all included in this.

**Scalable Architecture:** Creating a scalable architecture enables the smooth growth of user bases and virtual environments. This entails developing adaptable, modular systems that can handle growing scale and complexity.

The creation of Metaverse requires a complex technical infrastructure that includes networking solutions, data management systems, software platforms, and cutting-edge hardware. Developers may construct immersive, interactive, and scalable virtual worlds that push the limits of digital interaction by comprehending and skillfully putting these fundamental elements into practice. The Metaverse's underlying infrastructure will change as technology develops, opening the door for new discoveries and experiences in the digital frontier.

## ➢ Hardware Requirements: VR Headsets, AR Glasses, and More

The creation and functioning of the Metaverse significantly depend on cutting-edge technology that produces engaging and dynamic experiences. An overview of the crucial hardware elements required for Metaverse environments is given in this section, with a particular emphasis on VR headsets, AR glasses, and other relevant technologies.

### 1. Headsets for virtual reality (VR)

Virtual Reality (VR) headsets are intended to give consumers a completely realistic digital experience by simulating a real-world setting. These headgear is essential to virtual reality technology and is essential to the Metaverse.

**Important Elements:**

- **Displays:** Virtual reality headsets generally have wide-angle, high-resolution displays. The resolution and refresh rate of the display have a big impact on how clear and fluid the virtual experience seems. OLED or LCD displays with resolutions ranging from 1440p to 4K per eye are frequently used in modern headsets.

- **Sensors:** A variety of sensors are built into VR headsets to monitor user movements and interactions. These include devices that track the position and orientation of the head, such as magnetometers, gyroscopes, and accelerometers. Certain sophisticated headsets further employ external cameras or sensors to monitor the user's location inside a tangible area.

- **Audio:** By offering 3D soundscapes, integrated spatial audio systems in VR headsets improve immersion. Users can hear sounds coming from many directions thanks to this function, which enhances the realism of the experience. Certain headsets support external audio devices or come with built-in headphones.

- **Input Devices:** Motion controllers are a common feature of VR systems, enabling users to interact with the virtual world. These controllers have sensors to monitor button presses, gestures, and hand movements. Furthermore, haptic feedback is provided by certain systems to mimic physical feelings.

**Very Common VR Headsets:**

- **Oculus Quest 2:** A stand-alone virtual reality headset with a vast library of VR content, inside-out tracking, and high-resolution screens. It is a well-liked option for both developers and casual users because of its wireless capabilities and simplicity of use.

- **The HTC Vive Pro 2:** The Vive Pro 2, renowned for its accurate tracking and high-resolution screens, is frequently utilised for professional and high-end virtual reality applications. It has external base stations for precise tracking at the room scale.

- **PlayStation VR:** This headset, which is compatible with both the PlayStation 4 and PlayStation 5 systems, offers an immersive gaming experience with an emphasis on accessibility and PlayStation game integration.

## 2. Glasses for Augmented Reality (AR)

With the help of augmented reality (AR) glasses, users may interact with and contextualise digital content without being completely submerged in a virtual world. Applications that combine digital content with the real world require AR glasses.

**Important Elements:**

- **Displays:** Digital content is projected onto the user's field of view via AR glasses using waveguide technology or transparent displays. The augmented content's brightness and clarity are dependent on the display's quality. Certain AR glasses create high-resolution graphics by using holographic techniques or micro-displays.

**- Sensors and Cameras**: To enable features like gesture tracking and object recognition, AR glasses are outfitted with cameras and sensors that record their surroundings. These sensors are also useful for mapping the actual environment and lining up digital components with tangible objects.

**- Audio:** To provide audio without impairing the user's ability to hear their surroundings, some AR glasses come with tiny built-in speakers or bone conduction speakers. Users can hear information while still being aware of their surroundings because to this.

**- Processing Power:** In order to do computational activities, AR glasses frequently need to have onboard processing power or connectivity to external devices. Comfort and battery life are dependent on having processing solutions that are lightweight and effective.

**Common AR Eyewear:**

**- Microsoft HoloLens 2:** A popular augmented reality headset with sophisticated spatial computing features, such as hand tracking and high-resolution holograms. It is employed in many different industries for interactive applications, remote collaboration, and training.

**- Magic Leap 2:** Well-known for its emphasis on producing top-notch mixed reality encounters, Magic Leap 2 is appropriate for both creative and enterprise applications thanks to its broad field of vision, accurate hand tracking, and sophisticated spatial audio.

**- Elite Version of Google Glass:** Google Glass is a hands-free information and real-time data access device that is intended for industrial and enterprise use. It lets users stay focused on their tasks.

## 3. Extra Pieces of Hardware

In addition to VR headsets and AR glasses, the following hardware elements support the creation and use of the Metaverse:

- **Motion Tracking Systems:** These devices track a user's position and movements inside a physical area using external sensors or cameras. For more immersive interactions, devices such as the tracking sensors on the Oculus Rift or the base stations of the HTC Vive, for instance, offer exact room-scale tracking.

- **Haptic Feedback Devices:** In a virtual environment, haptic feedback devices, like gloves or vests, mimic physical feelings. These gadgets improve the feeling of touch and engagement with virtual objects by vibrating or providing force feedback.

## 4. High-Performance Graphics Cards and Computers

Considerable processing power is needed to render intricate virtual landscapes. Large-scale simulation management, real-time support for numerous users, and the creation and execution of intricate VR experiences all require strong GPUs and high-performance PCs.

**Networking Equipment:** Sturdy networking equipment is necessary for a smooth Metaverse experience. High-speed servers, switches, and routers that guarantee dependable connectivity and low latency between users and virtual environments fall under this category.

**Wearable Sensors:** Real-time information about a user's physical condition can be obtained by integrating wearable sensors, such as fitness trackers or biometric monitors, into the Metaverse. This data can improve interactive experiences and offer applications for wellness and health.

In order to create digital experiences that are seamless, interactive, and immersive, a variety of hardware requirements are necessary for Metaverse development. Each piece of hardware—VR headsets, AR glasses, and other pieces—has a distinct function in creating the intricate and captivating worlds that characterise the Metaverse. These hardware elements will develop more as technology progresses, allowing for increasingly complex and lifelike virtual experiences. In order to prepare for the future of digital engagement and connectivity, developers and users alike must comprehend and take advantage of these technologies.

## ➤ Platforms and Software for Metaverse Development

The creation, management, and optimisation of immersive virtual worlds in the vast Metaverse requires advanced software and development platforms. The main software and development tools—such as gaming engines, 3D modelling and animation software, AR SDKs, and blockchain platforms—that are necessary for creating the Metaverse are examined in this part.

1. **Game Engines**

The fundamental software tools for building and controlling interactive 3D environments in the Metaverse are called game engines. They offer the frameworks and tools required to manage user interactions, real-time rendering, physics simulations, and the creation of intricate virtual environments.

- **Unity:** One of the most popular game engines for creating Metaverse applications is Unity. It provides a flexible setting for making 2D and 3D material. Real-time rendering, physics simulation, and a large asset library are some of Unity's capabilities. Because of its cross-platform compatibility, it may be used for both conventional digital experiences and virtual reality.

**Key Features**: An extensive developer community, asset shop, cross-platform support, user-friendly interface, and plenty of documentation.

- **Unreal Engine:** Renowned for its potent tools and high-fidelity visuals, Unreal Engine was created by Epic Games. It is frequently used to create immersive virtual worlds and visually attractive virtual surroundings. With the help of Unreal Engine's Blueprint technology, developers can design intricate interactions without having a lot of coding experience.

**Key Features:** Large-scale scene management, high-level rendering, visual scripting in Blueprint, advanced graphics capabilities.

- **Godot:** An open-source gaming engine that provides a versatile and user-friendly development environment is Godot. It allows for both 2D and 3D game production and offers a special scene system that makes it easier to create intricate virtual environments. Godot is preferred because it is lightweight and simple to use.

**Key Features:** Support for multiple platforms, open-source, user-friendly, and a distinctive scene system.

## 2. Software for 3D Modelling and Animation

Specialised tools for 3D modelling and animation are needed to create dynamic, complex virtual environments. With the aid of these tools, developers may create environments, objects, and avatars with extreme accuracy and realism.

- **Blender:** Blender is a well-known open-source programme for 3D animation and modelling. It offers a full suite of tools for 3D object modelling, sculpting, texturing, and animation. Blender is renowned for its extensive feature set and adaptability, which includes support for simulation, rendering, and rigging.

**Key Features:** Rendering capabilities, a sizable user base, a wealth of modelling and animation tools, and open-source.

- **Autodesk Maya:** Often utilised in the video game and film sectors, Maya is a high-end 3D modelling and animation programme. It provides sophisticated modelling, rigging, texturing, and animating tools for intricate settings and people.

**Key Features:** Industry-standard software, sophisticated modelling and animation tools, and high-level rendering capabilities.

- **3ds Max:** Another Autodesk product, 3ds Max is renowned for its robust modelling and rendering tools and easy-to-use interface. It is frequently used to produce intricate 3D animations, visual effects, and models.

**Key Features:** Capabilities for animation, strong modelling and rendering tools, and an intuitive interface.

### 3. Spatially-Distinct SDKs

With the help of software development kits (SDKs) for augmented reality (AR), programmers may design apps that superimpose digital content on the physical world.

Frameworks and tools for incorporating augmented reality experiences into mobile devices and AR glasses are offered by these SDKs.

- **ARKit:** An SDK for generating augmented reality experiences for iOS devices, developed by Apple. With its capabilities, which include motion tracking, environment comprehension, and light estimate, developers may create captivating and dynamic augmented reality applications.

**Key Features:** Support for iOS devices, motion tracking, knowledge of the surrounding environment, and light estimate.

- **ARCore:** An SDK for Android device augmented reality applications, developed by Google. It provides ARKit-like functionality like augmented picture identification, motion tracking, and environmental comprehension.

**Key Features**: Support for Android smartphones, enhanced picture recognition, motion tracking, and environmental comprehension.

- **Vuforia:** Supporting both iOS and Android devices, Vuforia is a cross-platform AR SDK. It is appropriate for a variety of augmented reality applications since it offers tools for object tracking, picture recognition, and markerless AR experiences.

**Key Features:** Cross-platform compatibility, markerless AR, object tracking, and image recognition.

## 4. Distribution Networks

Because it facilitates decentralised transactions, digital asset management, and safe interactions, blockchain technology is essential to the Metaverse. The infrastructure for virtual currencies, NFTs (non-fungible tokens), and decentralised applications (dApps) is provided by blockchain platforms.

- **Ethereum:** A well-known blockchain platform that facilitates decentralised apps and smart contracts is Ethereum. It is extensively utilised in the Metaverse for the creation and administration of NFTs, virtual currencies, and other digital assets. Ethereum is a well-liked option for Metaverse projects because of its strong ecosystem and developer tools.

**Key Features**: A sizable developer community, dApp compatibility, NFT integration, and smart contracts.

**- Binance Smart Chain (BSC):** Binance Smart Chain is a blockchain platform that offers decentralised apps and smart contracts in a high-performance environment. Compared to Ethereum, it has faster processing times and reduced transaction costs, which makes it a desirable choice for Metaverse projects.

**Key Features:** Support for smart contracts, reduced transaction fees, and a high-performance environment.

**- Polygon (previously Matic Network):** Polygon is an Ethereum layer-2 scaling solution that lowers fees and speeds up transactions. It is utilised to create and implement scalable NFTs and dApps, hence resolving some of the Ethereum network's shortcomings.

Scalable infrastructure, lower transaction costs, and faster transactions are some of the Key Features.

**5. Extra Tools for Development**

A few more tools are necessary for Metaverse development in addition to the main software platforms and development tools:

**- Version Control Systems:** Programmes such as Git and GitHub facilitate the tracking of project progress, collaboration with other developers, and management of code modifications. Version management is essential for preserving the integrity of the code and promoting teamwork.

**- Integrated Development Environments (IDEs):** Code authoring and debugging environments are provided by IDEs like Visual Studio, JetBrains Rider, and Eclipse. These tools come with capabilities like debugging and code completion, and they support a number of programming languages.

- **Project Management Tools:** Jira, Trello, and Asana are a few examples of tools that help with tracking progress, organising development tasks, and organising teamwork. Timely delivery and effective collaboration are guaranteed by proficient project management.

Each of the several, specialised software and development platforms used in Metaverse development is essential to the creation and administration of immersive virtual worlds. Building intricate virtual worlds and interactive apps requires the use of frameworks and technologies that are provided by game engines, 3D modelling and animation tools, AR SDKs, and blockchain platforms. These technologies will develop further as the Metaverse goes on, adding new features and expanding the opportunities for digital participation and connection. Developers who want to influence the Metaverse's future must comprehend and use these programmes and development platforms effectively.

## ➢ Cloud Infrastructure and Networking

For flawless, immersive experiences in the field of Metaverse development, strong networking and cloud infrastructure are essential. In order to handle data, facilitate real-time interactions, and guarantee scalable, dependable connectivity, the Metaverse—a sizable digital environment that integrates virtual, augmented, and mixed realities—needs sophisticated technology. In-depth discussion of networking and cloud infrastructure fundamentals for Metaverse applications is provided in this section, with particular attention on scalability, data management, and connectivity.

### 1. The infrastructure for networking

The Metaverse's networking infrastructure makes it possible for people to communicate with one another and virtual worlds in real time, regardless of where they are physically located. Important elements of networking infrastructure consist of:

- **High-Speed Connectivity:** Due to the massive amounts of data transferred during immersive encounters, the Metaverse requires high-speed internet connections. High bandwidth and low latency are essential for minimising delays and guaranteeing seamless interactions. The implementation of technologies like 5G networks and fiber-optic internet is crucial to fulfilling these demands.

- **Low Latency:** The time interval between sending and receiving data is referred to as latency. Low latency is necessary in the Metaverse for real-time interactions like avatar movements and live virtual events. By processing data closer to the end user, strategies like content delivery networks (CDNs) and edge computing assist lower latency.

- **Material Delivery Networks (CDNs):** To improve performance and dependability, CDNs disperse material among several servers. Content delivery networks (CDNs) lower latency and increase access speeds for users worldwide by caching content at many geographic locations. Delivering high-resolution assets and real-time data in the Metaverse calls for this in particular.

**- Edge Computing:** Instead of depending exclusively on centralised cloud servers, edge computing processes data at or close to the source. By managing data locally, this method lowers latency and bandwidth use. Applications that need real-time reactions, including interactive virtual reality experiences and live virtual events, benefit from edge computing.

**- Network Security:** In the Metaverse, where user data and interactions are at risk, security is a crucial component of networking architecture. Strong security measures, such intrusion detection systems, firewalls, and encryption, can be put into place to help defend against online threats and guarantee the integrity of data transfers.

**- Scalability:** The networking infrastructure needs to grow with the Metaverse as it draws in additional users. In order to accommodate growing traffic and user needs, this entails improving network hardware, expanding bandwidth, and optimising network settings.

## 2. Cloud Computing

The processing power, storage, and services required to meet the Metaverse's resource-intensive and dynamic needs are provided via cloud infrastructure. Important components of cloud infrastructure consist of:

**Cloud Computing Platforms:** Scalable and adaptable resources are available for Metaverse development on popular cloud computing platforms such as Google Cloud, Microsoft Azure, and Amazon Web Services (AWS). These systems let developers create, implement, and maintain virtual environments by offering virtual machines, storage options, and other services.

**AWS (Amazon Web Services):** Database management (RDS), storage (S3), and processing power (EC2) are just a few of the many services that AWS provides. Because of its extensive worldwide data centre network, which guarantees high availability and dependability, AWS is a good choice for managing complex Metaverse applications.

**Microsoft Azure:** Azure offers a range of services, including databases, virtual computers, and artificial intelligence capabilities. Because of Azure's support for hybrid cloud solutions, developers may construct and manage complex Metaverse settings with flexibility through flexible interaction with on-premises systems.

**Google Cloud:** Google Cloud provides robust machine learning, data storage, and processing capability. The Metaverse requires real-time data processing and high-performance applications, which are supported by its infrastructure.

**Scalable Storage Solutions:** Virtual assets, user interactions, and environmental data are just a few of the massive volumes of data produced by the Metaverse. Developers can efficiently manage and retrieve data thanks to cloud storage solutions, which offer scalable and dependable storage alternatives. Different forms of data are handled via solutions like databases, block storage, and object storage (like Amazon S3).

**Database Management:** In the Metaverse, databases are necessary for the management of user information, virtual assets, and application states. Relational databases (like Amazon RDS, Azure SQL Database) and NoSQL databases (like MongoDB, DynamoDB) are among the database options provided by cloud platforms. Efficient data retrieval and management are guaranteed by these databases.

**Load Balancing**: To guarantee peak performance and avoid overload, load balancing divides incoming traffic among several servers. Ensuring the reliability and responsiveness of Metaverse apps is critical, particularly during periods of high usage.

**Disaster Recovery:** In the event of malfunctions or outages, cloud infrastructure offers disaster recovery options to guarantee data integrity and availability. Replication, failover, and automated backups all reduce downtime and provide data protection.

**Development and Deployment Tools:** A variety of tools for development and deployment are available on cloud platforms, including pipelines for continuous integration and deployment (CI/CD), container orchestration (like Kubernetes), and monitoring tools. With the use of these tools, developers may more effectively manage and grow their projects as they design, test, and implement Metaverse applications.

### 3. Analytics and Data Management

Optimising speed and user experience in the Metaverse requires effective data management and analytics:

**Data Analytics:** Developers can learn more about how users interact with the Metaverse by analysing user interactions, behaviour, and performance indicators. Useful data is provided by tools like Google Analytics, AWS Analytics, and Azure Monitor, which may be leveraged to enhance application performance and customer happiness.

**Real-Time Data Processing:** Applications that need to get feedback right away, such as interactive experiences and live virtual events, depend on real-time data processing. Developers can react to user activities in real-time by processing and analysing streaming data thanks to technologies like AWS Kinesis and Apache Kafka.

**Data Privacy and Compliance:** In the Metaverse, it is essential to guarantee data privacy and compliance with laws like the California Consumer Privacy Act (CCPA) and the General Data Protection Regulation (GDPR). Encryption and access restrictions are two examples of data protection methods that can be put into place to assist protect user information and ensure legal compliance.

The creation and functioning of the Metaverse depend heavily on networking and cloud computing infrastructure. Robust networking solutions, low latency, and high-speed connectivity guarantee seamless and rapid user interactions, and cloud computing platforms offer the scalable resources required to administer and implement intricate virtual environments. Efficient analytics and data management also improve Metaverse performance and user experience. These infrastructure elements will develop together with technology, enabling the Metaverse and its numerous uses to flourish and flourish. Developers and organisations that want to create and maintain immersive, interactive digital environments must comprehend and use these technologies.

# Chapter Three

# Constructing Virtual Environments

The main goal of Metaverse development is to create dynamic, immersive virtual worlds. Within the Metaverse, virtual environments are places where people can connect, explore, socialise, and take part in a variety of activities. A combination of technology, creativity, and design concepts are used in the construction of these worlds. This manual examines the essential elements and procedures needed to create engaging virtual worlds.

## 1. Planning and Conceptualization

Conception and planning are the first steps in creating a virtual world. In this stage, the goal, target market, and salient characteristics of the virtual environment are defined.

**Purpose and Objectives:** Clearly state what the virtual environment is meant to accomplish. Is it for trade, education, social contact, or gaming? The design and development process will be guided by an understanding of the main goal.

**Target Audience:** Determine the preferences of the intended audience. This will have an impact on the environment's appearance, usability, and interactivity.

**Core Features:** List the main attributes and features. If one were to create a virtual mall, for instance, features might include interactive product displays, virtual stores, and payment mechanisms.

**Storyboard and Mockups:** To see the layout, user flow, and important environment components, create storyboards and mockups. This aids in idea refinement and guarantees that everyone involved understands the project.

## 2. Tools for Design and Development

Choosing the appropriate tools is essential to creating productive virtual environments. These tools include asset libraries, 3D modelling programmes, and gaming engines.

**Game Engines:** As was previously mentioned, interactive and aesthetically stunning virtual worlds can only be made with the help of game engines like Unity and Unreal Engine. They provide functions including processing user input, physics simulations, and real-time rendering.

**3D Modelling Software:** To create intricate 3D models of objects, characters, and environments, use programmes like Blender, Autodesk Maya, and 3ds Max. The foundation of the virtual world is made up of these models.

**Asset Libraries:** To find pre-made 3D models, textures, and animations, use asset libraries and marketplaces.

This can save expenses and expedite the development process considerably.

**Collaborative Tools:** To manage projects, monitor progress, and improve team communication, use collaborative tools like Asana, Jira, or Trello.

## 3. Design and Layout of the Environment

One of the most important steps is designing the virtual environment's structure and layout. It entails designing a space that is both practical and aesthetically pleasing to improve user experience.

**World Building:** Begin by creating the environment's general composition and structure. This entails specifying the topography, architectural style, and spatial configuration of important components.

**Textures and Materials:** To make 3D models look realistic, add textures and materials to them. Materials determine how objects interact with light, whereas textures contribute elements like colour, patterns, and surface characteristics.

**Lighting and Shadows:** Use lighting to set the right tone and atmosphere. The environment's depth and visual attractiveness are improved by realistic lighting. To create depth and realism, use shadows.

**Sound Design:** To improve immersion, use background music and sound effects. Through the provision of aural signals and the enhancement of ambiance, sound design can have a substantial impact on the user experience.

**4. User Experience and Interactivity**

One characteristic that sets virtual environments apart is interactivity. Creating user-friendly and captivating interactions is crucial to retaining users' attention.

**User Interface (UI):** Create an intuitive user interface that enables users to interact with items, retrieve information, and explore the surroundings. This covers buttons, menus, and icons.

**User Input Handling:** Put in place systems to manage user inputs, including VR controllers, keyboard and mouse clicks. Make sure that communication flows easily and quickly.

**Physics and Movement:** To replicate object behaviour and movement, incorporate accurate physics. As a result, interactions feel more natural and immersion is improved.

**Animations:** Animated objects and characters have life of their own. Animations can offer dynamic elements to an environment by varying from basic movements to intricate behaviours.

## 5. Performance and Optimisation

For a flawless user experience, performance must be guaranteed. Virtual environments need to be optimised for a range of device types.

**Performance Testing:** To find and fix problems with responsiveness, load times, and frame rates, do performance testing. Track performance measurements by utilising profiling tools.

**Level of Detail (LOD)**: Use LOD methods to simplify far-off objects, enhancing performance without compromising visual appeal.

**Asset Optimisation:** To minimise file sizes and speed up loading times, optimise 3D models, textures, and animations. Texture compression, mesh simplification, and asset efficiency are some of the techniques.

**Network Optimisation:** Make sure to use the network effectively in multiplayer settings to reduce latency and offer a seamless online experience. Effective synchronisation and data compression are two methods.

## 6. Evaluation and Input

For the virtual environment to be improved and made sure it fulfils user expectations, extensive testing and feedback are necessary.

**Beta Testing:** Get user input on usability, performance, and overall experience by doing beta testing with a set of users. This aids in locating problems and potential improvement areas.

**Usability Testing:** Assess the usability of the navigation and interaction by conducting usability testing. Make sure the environment is intuitive for users to comprehend and interact with.

**Iterative Improvement:** Make adjustments based on user feedback. Iteratively improve the environment by taking user feedback and test findings into consideration.

## 7. Upgrading and Upkeep

Deployment and continuing maintenance come next after the virtual environment is finished.

**Deployment Platforms:** Select the right platforms, including web browsers, mobile devices, or VR headsets, for deployment. Verify compatibility and perform platform-specific optimisation.

**Cloud Services:** To host and administer the virtual environment, make use of cloud services. Cloud platforms make updates and maintenance easier and offer scalable resources.

**Regular Updates:** Make sure the environment is updated often to introduce new features, address bugs, and enhance functionality. Users find the atmosphere exciting and fresh because of regular improvements.

**User Support:** Help users get around and solve problems by offering user support. This improves user retention and satisfaction.

The process of creating virtual worlds for the Metaverse is intricate and multidimensional, integrating design, technology, and user experience concepts. Every stage, from planning and ideation to implementation and maintenance, calls for in-depth knowledge and careful thought. Developers may construct engaging virtual environments that attract consumers by utilising appropriate tools and strategies. The creation of virtual environments will become more and more possible as technology develops, opening up new avenues for creativity and innovation in the Metaverse.

## ➢ 3D Modeling and Graphics

The creation of virtual worlds for the Metaverse starts with 3D modelling and visuals. In order to create realistic and engrossing visual experiences, they entail meticulously modelling objects, characters, and settings in three dimensions. These models are then produced. The fundamentals of 3D modelling and graphics are covered in this section, along with methods, tools, and best practices for producing 3D material of the highest calibre.

**1. Providing an Overview of 3D Modelling**

Creating a mathematical representation of a three-dimensional object is known as 3D modelling. The visual components that make up virtual environments are created through this process, which is essential.

**Fundamental Ideas:**
**- Vertices, Edges, and Faces:** The essential components of three-dimensional models. In three-dimensional space, vertices are points, edges are lines that join vertices, and faces are flat surfaces that are encircled by edges.

- **Polygons**: Triangles and quadrilaterals, which make up the object's mesh, are the most common polygons used in the construction of 3D models.

- **Meshes:** A mesh is an assembly of faces, edges, and vertices that determines a three-dimensional object's shape.

**Modelling Methods:**
- **Box Modelling:** consists of beginning with a basic geometric shape (such as a cube) and adding details to refine it.

- **Sculpting:** This method, which is similar to sculpting clay, frequently makes use of ZBrush tools and permits the creation of organic shapes and intricate details.

- **Procedural Modelling:** Produces intricate models through the application of algorithms; excellent for modelling terrain and natural settings.

## 2. 3D Modelling Tools

For 3D modelling, a wide variety of software packages are available, each with special features and functionalities. These are a handful of the most well-liked ones:

- **Blender:** An open-source programme that offers a full range of tools for texturing, modelling, sculpting, and animating. Due to its affordability and adaptability, blenders are utilised extensively.

- **Autodesk Maya:** A high-end tool widely utilised in the video game, film, and television industries. Advanced modelling, texturing, rigging, and animation features are available with Maya.

- **3ds Max:** Another Autodesk product, 3ds Max is popular in game development and architectural visualisation due to its strong modelling tools.

- **ZBrush:** An advanced digital sculpting and painting tool that is perfect for producing incredibly intricate organic models. ZBrush is a popular tool for modelling characters.

- **Cinema 4D**: A strong modelling and animation tool that is popular in motion graphics and visual effects. It is easy to use.

**3. Shading and Texturing**

Texturing and shading are used to add colour, texture, and material qualities to a 3D object after it has been generated. Reaching realism requires taking this key step.

- **UV Mapping:** The technique of projecting the texture of a 2D image onto a 3D object. To precisely apply textures, UV mapping entails unwrapping the 3D model into a 2D space.

- **Textures:** Pictures that are layered onto a 3D model's surface to add surface diversity, colour, and detail. Diffuse (colour), Normal (bump mapping), and Specular (reflectivity) are common textures.

- **Materials and Shaders:** Specify how the model's surface responds to light. Textures are combined with qualities such as glossiness, transparency, and reflection in materials. Programmes called shaders compute these attributes during rendering.

**4. Display**

The process of turning a 3D model into a finished picture or animation is called rendering. For realistic images, light simulation is used.

**Real-Time Rendering:** Used in interactive applications where fast image rendering is necessary to maintain a seamless user experience, such as virtual reality and video games. Real-time rendering is the area of expertise for game engines such as Unreal Engine and Unity.

**Offline Rendering**: Used in movies and high-end visual effects, where the goal is to achieve the best possible quality rather than rendering time. For offline rendering, programmes like Autodesk Arnold and Blender's Cycles are utilised.

**Ray Tracing:** A rendering method that produces realistic visuals by mimicking the behaviour of light. Although ray tracing requires a lot of processing power, it yields very lifelike lighting effects, such as shadows and reflections.

## 5. Rigging and Animation

3D models come to life through animation, which adds motion and behaviours. Setting up a model's skeleton so that animators may work with it is known as rigging.

**Rigging:** The process of putting together a 3D model's skeleton, also known as a rig. The model's movement is controlled by a system of joints and bones called a rig.

Tools with advanced rigging capabilities include Blender and Autodesk Maya.

**Keyframe Animation:** This type of animation involves arranging a model's key poses at predetermined intervals, with the programme interpolating the motion in between.

**Motion Capture:** Using 3D models, real actors' movements are captured. Production companies that create video games and films frequently employ this method.

**Physics-Based Animation:** This type of animation uses physics simulations to produce realistic movements, including figures interacting with their surroundings or material draping.

**6. Game Engine Integration**

Game engines may generate dynamic virtual environments by integrating 3D models and animations.

Real-time scene construction, rendering, and interaction are made possible by game engines.

**Unity:** A popular gaming engine with cross-platform compatibility. Unity provides tools for texture application, animation creation, and 3D model importation. For interactivity, it also offers scripting capabilities.

**Unreal Engine:** Widely used in virtual production and game development, Unreal Engine is renowned for its excellent graphics and real-time rendering capabilities. It can handle intricate animations, accurate lighting, and intricate surroundings.

## 7. Performance Optimisation

For 3D models and surroundings to function well across a range of devices—particularly in real-time applications like virtual reality and games—they must be optimised.

**Level of Detail (LOD):** Building several models with differing degrees of intricacy. Depending on how far the model is from the camera, the game engine will automatically alternate between these variants.

**Texture Compression:** Lowering texture file sizes to enhance performance and loading times. Mipmapping is one technique that helps preserve texture quality at various distances.

**Polygon Reduction:** Lowering a model's polygon count to boost performance without appreciably sacrificing visual appeal.

Using 3D modelling and graphics is essential for building virtual worlds for the Metaverse. A combination of technical know-how and artistic abilities are needed to create realistic and detailed 3D models, from the first concept to the finished render. Developers are able to create captivating, dynamic worlds that enthral consumers by utilising sophisticated tools and approaches. The possibilities for 3D modelling and graphics in the Metaverse will grow as technology develops further, presenting fresh chances for ingenuity and creativity. It is essential for everyone participating in the creation of virtual environments to comprehend and become proficient in these principles.

## ➢ Crafting Immersive Metaverse Experiences

The process of crafting immersive experiences in the Metaverse involves a complex fusion of technology, narrative, interactivity, and design principles. The goal of these encounters is to fully engross consumers and give them a sense of immersion in the virtual world. A number of crucial elements must be considered in order to achieve immersion, such as user interaction, narrative depth, and sensory engagement.

## 1. Emotional Involvement

In order to create a realistic impression of the virtual world, sensory engagement is essential for immersion. This encompasses aspects that are tactile, aural, and occasionally visual.

**Visual Immersion:** Detailed textures, realistic lighting, and excellent graphics all support a visually immersive experience. Realistic rendering can be improved with techniques like high dynamic range (HDR) rendering and ray tracing. It is crucial to maintain consistency in the visual design, which includes the smooth transition of items and surroundings.

**Auditory Immersion:** An immersive experience is greatly influenced by sound design. This comprises directed audio, ambient sounds, and sound effects that blend in with the ambiance and activity of the surrounding area. The use of spatial audio technology improves the sense of depth and space by simulating the real-world propagation of sound.

**Haptic Feedback:** Haptic feedback adds a tactile element to VR and AR experiences. The feeling of presence is enhanced by gadgets like haptic suits and VR controllers, which produce real-world physical sensations in line with virtual interactions.

## 2. Deep Storyline

Users can be drawn into and maintained in a virtual environment by an engaging story. To establish a strong bond with the user, the plot should be engaging, dynamic, and tailored to them.

**Storytelling:** Create a compelling narrative and backstory that readers can delve into and shape. Immersion can be greatly increased by using dynamic storytelling, in which the story changes based on the choices and actions of the user.

**NPCs and Characters:** Authentic dialogue and well-crafted non-player characters (NPCs) may breathe life into the setting. An experience that is more dynamic and captivating is enhanced by AI-driven NPCs that react intelligently to user interactions.

**Universe-Building:** Construct a coherent, well-researched universe with a distinct history, society, and set of laws. This facilitates users' ability to suspend disbelief and get totally absorbed in the setting.

### 3. Interaction with Users

An essential element of immersive experiences is interaction. It should be easy and natural for users to interact with the virtual world.

**Intuitive Controls:** Create controls and user interfaces that are simple to understand and operate. To enable natural interactions in VR, think about utilising gesture detection and hand tracking.

**Responsive Environment:** Make sure that the surroundings respond meaningfully to user actions. This includes real-time feedback, dynamic lighting changes, and interactions based on physics.

**Customisation**: Give people the option to personalise their settings, experiences, and avatars. Personalisation fosters a sense of control and ownership in users, which boosts engagement.

## 4. Conversation with Others

Social interaction, which enables users to communicate and work together with others in the virtual environment, improves immersion.

**Multiplayer Experiences:** Create settings that facilitate group exploration and communication between users. These can include competitive challenges, social settings, and cooperative tasks.

**Text and Voice Communication:** Include text and voice chat features to help users communicate with one another. Realistic speech is improved by spatial voice chat, in which the speaker's voice comes from their direction.

**Social Presence:** Include elements like lifelike avatars, body language, and facial emotions that improve the experience of being in the company of people.

## 5. Technological Points to Remember

For experiences to be seamless and immersive, technical elements are essential. Hardware, software, and performance optimization are a few of these.

**Hardware Requirements:** Make sure the setting is appropriate for the intended hardware, such as regular screens, AR glasses, or VR headsets. In particular in virtual reality, maintaining immersion requires high frame rates and little latency.

**Performance Optimisation:** To guarantee fluid gameplay, optimise the assets, lighting, and physics. High performance can be maintained with the use of strategies like texture compression, level of detail (LOD) management, and effective scripting.

**Network Infrastructure:** To reduce latency and guarantee synchronised interactions, a strong network infrastructure is required for multiplayer experiences. To manage the processing load and offer scalable resources, use cloud services.

## 6. Design Principles

More immersive and user-friendly environments can be produced by following specific design concepts.

**Cohesion and Consistency:** Make sure that the interaction mechanics, sound design, and visual style are all consistent. Users can comprehend and traverse the environment more readily when it is designed cohesively.

**User-Centered Design:** By doing user testing and obtaining feedback, put the user experience front and centre. To boost immersion and usability, iteratively update the environment based on user feedback.

**Accessibility:** Make sure that a variety of users, including those with disabilities, can easily interact with the environment. Options for movement, visual, and hearing impairments are included in this.

## 7. Introductory Experience Examples

**Virtual Reality (VR) Games:** With dynamic gameplay, lifelike graphics, and captivating stories, games like "Beat Sabre" and "Half-Life: Alyx" offer incredibly immersive experiences.

**Social VR Platforms:** By providing social areas where users may mingle, play games, and go to events, platforms such as VRChat and Rec Room help users feel present and part of a community.

**Training Simulations:** The military, aviation, and healthcare industries all employ VR and AR for training simulations. Through hands-on participation, these simulators enhance immersion by offering realistic scenarios for practice and learning.

**Virtual Museums and Galleries**: Users can explore exhibits and engage with informative displays through virtual tours of museums and art galleries, which offer immersive educational experiences.

Technology, design, and user interaction must be carefully balanced in order to create immersive experiences in the Metaverse. Developers may create virtual environments that enthral and immerse users by emphasising technical optimisation, social dynamics, user interaction, narrative depth, and sensory engagement. The possibility of developing even more fascinating and lifelike Metaverse experiences will increase as technology develops, presenting fresh chances for creativity and interaction. Anyone working on creating immersive virtual environments needs to comprehend and put these ideas into practice.

## ➢ Designing User Experience (UX) and User Interface (UI)

In the Metaverse, designing user interfaces (UI) and user experiences (UX) is essential to building interactive and hospitable virtual worlds. UX design includes the entire experience and the way people feel when engaging with these environments, whereas UI design concentrates on the layout and interactive features. Designing a user interface and user experience well can greatly improve immersion, usability, and enjoyment.

**1. UI Design Fundamentals**

Making user-interactive interfaces is the goal of UI design. This can contain menus, buttons, controls, and other interactive features within the Metaverse.

- **Simplicity and Clarity:** To prevent overwhelming users, the interface should be straightforward and uncomplicated. A glance understanding and intuitiveness are key components.

- **Consistency:** Users can navigate the environment more readily when design components (such as colours, typefaces, and icons) are used consistently. Interactive features must behave consistently as well.

- **Visual Hierarchy**: Direct users' attention to the most crucial components first by using visual hierarchy. Positioning, size, and colour contrast can all help achieve this.

- **Feedback:** Respond to user actions promptly and clearly. For instance, buttons that are interactive should seem differently whether viewed from the side or clicked.

## 2. UX Design Principles

The general impression of the user's contact with the environment is what UX design is all about. It entails comprehending the requirements, actions, and feelings of the user.

- **User-Centered Design:** Pay attention to the end users' requirements, preferences, and constraints. This strategy guarantees that the setting is customised to deliver the greatest experience.

- **Ease of Use:** The setting ought to be simple to use and intuitive. It should not be necessary for users to read through lengthy instructions in order to interact with the virtual environment.

- **Accessibility:** Make sure the environment is usable by persons with a range of disabilities by designing with accessibility in mind. This provides options for voice commands, several input methods, and font size adjustment.

- **Engagement:** Provide captivating experiences to maintain consumers' attention and involvement.

Interactive components, gripping stories, and accommodating settings can accomplish this.

**3. The Process of UI/UX Design**

There are various stages involved in the design process, ranging from preliminary research to final testing and iteration.

**Research and Analysis:** Gather information about the needs, preferences, and pain points of the target audience through user research. Usability studies, interviews, and surveys may be a part of this.

**Wireframing and Prototyping:** To visualise and test the design, create wireframes and prototypes. Prototypes are more interactive and detailed representations of the interface, whereas wireframes are simple layouts that depict its structure.

**Design and Development:** Produce the interactive components and graphic design. Choosing fonts, colour schemes, icons, and other design components are all part of this process.

**Testing and Iteration:** Put the design to the test on actual users to get their input and pinpoint areas that need work. Use this input to inform future design iterations that will improve user pleasure and usability.

**4. UI/UX Design Tools**

The UI/UX design process can be aided by a number of tools, from wireframing to final design and prototyping.

- **Sketch**: A widely used programme for designing user interfaces and wireframes. It is renowned for being easy to use and having strong vector editing skills.

- **Figma:** A real-time collaborative design tool hosted on the cloud. Figma is an excellent tool for developing prototypes and gathering team member input.

- **Adobe XD:** A flexible interface design and prototype tool. Because it can be integrated with other Adobe products, Adobe XD is a very useful tool for designers.

- **InVision:** A tool for prototyping that enables designers to produce interactive mockups and get stakeholders' and users' input.

**5. Creating Content for Various Devices**

There are several ways to enter the Metaverse: via VR headsets, AR glasses, and conventional screens, among others. Every gadget has unique UI/UX design factors to take into account.

- **VR Headsets:** Spatial interfaces and user-friendly controls should be the main priorities of VR design. To create a natural experience, make use of voice commands, hand tracking, and gaze-based interactions.

- **AR Glasses:** When designing augmented reality, real-world and virtual aspects should be blended together. Make sure virtual elements don't block the user's view, and make use of interactions that are aware of context.

- **Traditional Screens:** Make sure the interface is flexible and adjusts to various screen sizes and resolutions for users who are accessing the Metaverse via PCs or mobile devices.

**6. UI/UX Design Challenges for the Metaverse**

When it comes to UI/UX design, the Metaverse has different issues than standard programmes.

- **Usability vs. Immersion**: It might be difficult to strike a balance between usability and immersive experiences. Interface designers have to make sure that functionality doesn't interfere with the user's sense of presence.

- **Differing User tastes:** Individuals may differ in their tastes and degree of experience with virtual reality and augmented reality. Adaptability and flexibility are necessary when designing for a diverse user base.

- **Technological Limitations:** The design process may be impacted by present software and hardware constraints. To create interfaces that are effective, designers have to operate within these limitations.

- **Privacy and Security:** In the Metaverse, protecting user privacy and security is essential. Interfaces should have strong security features and unambiguous information about how data is used.

## 7. UI/UX Design Best Practices in the Metaverse

Think about the following best practices while creating UI/UX in the Metaverse to make it compelling and effective:

- **User Testing:** Test the design frequently with actual users to find problems and get input. User testing aids in confirming that the design satisfies the target audience's requirements and expectations.

- **Accessibility:** Give accessibility top priority to make sure that everyone can engage with the surroundings. This entails taking motor, visual, and auditory deficits into account.

- **Contextual Interactions**: Create interactions that are appropriate for the virtual environment's context. To improve immersion, for instance, use voice instructions and organic motions.

- **Minimise Distractions:** Steer clear of extraneous details and clutter that could divert consumers. Concentrate on developing a simple, user-friendly interface that improves the user experience.

- **Consistency:** Keep interactions and design components consistent. Users can comprehend and traverse the environment more readily when the design is consistent.

In order to provide accessible and interesting experiences in the Metaverse, UI and UX design are essential. Through the implementation of user-centered design, consistency, and clarity, developers may produce interfaces that improve usability and immersion. Designing for VR, AR, and other devices presents special problems that need for an adaptable, iterative process with ongoing testing and feedback. Effective UI/UX design will be essential in determining how the Metaverse develops in the future and making sure that users can connect, explore, and engage with it with ease as technology advances.

# Chapter Four

# Building Applications for the Metaverse

The process of creating applications for the Metaverse is intricate and ever-changing, incorporating aspects of blockchain, virtual reality, augmented reality, artificial intelligence, and the Internet of Things (IoT). Developers are challenged to create immersive, dynamic, and highly engaging applications that push the frontiers of technology and user experience, as the Metaverse concept continues to advance. The main ideas and factors to be taken into account when creating Metaverse applications will be discussed in this article.

## 1. Getting to Know the Metaverse

The merging of physically persistent virtual reality with virtually improved physical reality has produced a communal virtual shared world known as the Metaverse. It encompasses the internet, augmented reality, and all virtual worlds. Applications in the Metaverse can be anything from business and trade to social media, gaming, healthcare, and education.

**2. Primary Technologies**

Several key technologies must be thoroughly understood in order to develop Metaverse applications:

- **Virtual Reality (VR):** VR offers completely immersive experiences; headgear such as the Oculus Rift or HTC Vive are frequently needed. 3D settings that users can interact with in a way that seems realistic are what developers need to create.

- **Augmented Reality (AR):** AR requires gadgets like smartphones or AR glasses (e.g., Microsoft HoloLens) to overlay digital information onto the physical world. Applications and the physical world must work together harmoniously.

- **Blockchain:** The Metaverse's digital ownership and safe, transparent transactions are guaranteed by blockchain technology. For applications including NFTs, decentralised governance, and virtual economies, it is essential.

**- Artificial Intelligence (AI):** AI is the driving force behind data-driven insights, personalised experiences, and intelligent NPCs. Algorithms for machine learning can improve user interactions and dynamically change their surroundings.

**- Internet of Things (IoT):** IoT gadgets allow for real-time data sharing and engagement by establishing a connection between the physical world and the Metaverse. IoT applications can provide more intelligent, context-aware user experiences.

### 3. Tools and Platforms for Development

Choosing the appropriate development platform and tools is essential when creating applications for the Metaverse. Several well-liked choices consist of:

- **Unity:** A popular and adaptable game engine that facilitates the creation of AR and VR content. Unity is renowned for its cross-platform capabilities and provides a comprehensive collection of tools for building interactive 3D environments.

- **Unreal Engine:** Well-known for its high-fidelity visuals, Unreal Engine is an effective tool for creating virtual reality experiences that are fully immersive. It offers sophisticated capabilities for physics simulation, photorealistic rendering, and interactive real-time graphics.

- **Blender:** A free and open-source programme for 3D modelling and animation is Blender. Blender is an indispensable tool for producing environments, animations, and assets for apps used in the Metaverse.

- **Vuforia:** A top AR platform that enables the creation of AR experiences by developers. Vuforia provides tools for object tracking, picture recognition, and spatial mapping and supports a number of different devices.

- **WebXR:** A web standard called **WebXR** makes it possible to have VR and AR experiences from within web browsers. Cross-platform, accessible Metaverse application development requires WebXR.

## 4. Creating Immersions Through Design

In the Metaverse, creating immersive experiences requires combining interactivity, storytelling, and sensory engagement.

- **Narrative Design:** Create an engaging plot or setting to entice users to enter the virtual world. Emotional connections and increased engagement can be achieved through rich storytelling.

- **Interactive Elements:** Include interactive features that let users change the surroundings and results. This can feature dynamic environments, puzzles, and interactions with NPCs.

- **Sensory Engagement:** To improve immersion, make

use of tactile, aural, and visual feedback. Experiences can be made more realistic and captivating by utilising haptic feedback devices, spatial audio, and high-quality images.

## 5. Designing User Experience (UX) and User Interface (UI)

In Metaverse apps, user engagement and pleasure are largely dependent on well-designed UI and UX.

- **Intuitive Navigation:** Create user-friendly, intuitive navigation solutions. It should be easy for users to move around and engage with the surroundings.

- **Consistency:** Retain uniformity in feedback, interactions, and visual design. Consistent design cues ease consumers' discomfort and lighten their cognitive strain.

- **Accessibility:** Make sure users of different abilities can utilise the application. This includes functions like text size adjustments, voice commands, and many input options.

## 6. Optimisation of Performance

Delivering seamless and responsive experiences requires performance optimisation, particularly in VR and AR applications.

- **Efficient Asset Management:** To lessen the computational burden, optimise 3D models, textures, and animations. Employ level of detail (LOD) strategies for efficient resource management.

- **Rendering Techniques:** To increase performance, use sophisticated rendering techniques like baked lighting, occlusion culling, and frustum culling.

- **Latency Reduction:** Reduce latency to guarantee real-time interaction (Latency Reduction). Input handling, frame rates, and network connection must all be optimised for this.

## 7. Privacy and Security

In the Metaverse, where users interact with sensitive data and digital assets, security and privacy are critical concerns.

- **Data Protection:** To safeguard user data and transactions, put strong encryption and data protection procedures in place.

- **User Authentication:** To improve security, use blockchain-based identity verification and multi-factor authentication.

- **Privacy Policies:** Provide consumers with control over their data and establish explicit privacy policies. Openness on the gathering and application of data fosters trust.

## 8. Strategies for Monetization

Depending on the type of application, monetization

tactics for Metaverse applications can differ significantly.

- **In-App Purchases:** Charge for in-app virtual items, upgrades, and personalisation choices.

- **Subscription Models:** Provide access to premium features, material, or services through a subscription model.

- **Advertising:** Incorporate discreet advertising into the online space. This can include virtual billboards, sponsored events, and branded areas.

- **Virtual Real Estate:** Market and rent out virtual real estate located in the Metaverse. This is a market that is expanding, especially for virtual worlds and social media platforms.

### 9. Examination and Repetition

Iteration and continuous testing are essential to the

development of effective Metaverse apps.

- **User Testing:** To get input and find usability problems, do frequent user testing. Surveys, focus groups, and beta testing are a few examples of this.

- **Performance Testing:** Verify the application's performance and stability under a range of circumstances. Compatibility, load, and stress testing are all included in this.

- **Iteration:** Make iterative improvements to the application based on user feedback and test findings. This procedure can be streamlined with the use of agile development approaches.

Creating apps for the Metaverse is a thrilling and difficult task that calls for a fusion of creative design, technical know-how, and user-centered thinking. Developers can produce engrossing and captivating virtual environments by utilising key technology, selecting appropriate development platforms, and emphasising immersive experiences. The likelihood of success is further increased by paying attention to UI/UX design, performance optimisation, security, and monetization techniques. There are countless chances for creative and significant uses as the Metaverse expands and changes, providing new avenues for individuals to engage, educate, and amuse themselves in virtual spaces.

## ➢ Development of VR and AR Applications

The way we interact with digital information has been completely transformed by virtual reality (VR) and augmented reality (AR), which have brought previously unimaginable immersive and interactive experiences into the real world. As these technologies advance, developers will have several chances to create cutting-edge apps for a variety of industries, such as gaming, real estate, healthcare, education, and more. This article offers a thorough examination of the fundamental ideas, resources, and industry best practices involved in creating VR and AR apps.

## 1. Knowing VR from AR

**Virtual Reality (VR):** With VR headgear such as the Oculus Rift, HTC Vive, or PlayStation VR, users can interact with a completely immersive digital environment. In a virtual environment, users are fully submerged and feel as though they are physically present.

**Augmented Reality (AR):** AR improves a user's perspective of their environment by superimposing digital information on the real world. This is made possible by gadgets like tablets, smartphones, and augmented reality glasses like Google Glass or Microsoft HoloLens. AR apps use real-time blending to combine digital and physical elements.

## 2. Principles and Fundamental Technologies

Creating VR and AR apps requires a thorough grasp of a number of fundamental technologies and ideas, including:

- **3D Modelling and Animation:** VR and AR applications require realistic and captivating 3D models and animations. Commonly used tools include Blender, Autodesk Maya, and Cinema 4D.

- **Spatial Computing:** To precisely position digital objects in augmented reality, spatial computing entails comprehending and mapping the physical surroundings. It is essential to have technologies such as simultaneous localization and mapping (SLAM).

- **Human-Computer Interaction (HCI):** It's critical to create natural and intuitive interfaces for people to engage with augmented or virtual environments. Voice instructions, haptic feedback, and gesture recognition are a few examples of this.

- **Rendering and Graphics:** Creating immersive experiences requires rendering and graphics of the highest calibre. Performance is maximised by employing strategies like level of detail (LOD), occlusion culling, and ray tracing.

## 3. Platforms and Tools for Development

Selecting the appropriate platforms and development tools is essential for the success of VR and AR apps.

- **Unity:** A flexible game engine that's popular in VR and AR games. Unity is a cross-platform software that provides an extensive toolkit for building interactive 3D worlds.

- **Unreal Engine:** Another well-liked option for VR creation, Unreal Engine is renowned for its high-fidelity graphics. It offers sophisticated capabilities for interactive real-time rendering and photorealistic rendering.

- **ARKit and ARCore:** Apple and Google, respectively, offer these AR development platforms. On iOS and Android devices, ARKit and ARCore provide tools and frameworks for building augmented reality experiences.

- **Microsoft Mixed Reality:** This platform supports HoloLens and Windows Mixed Reality headsets, and it offers tools for creating VR and AR applications.

**4. Creating Immersions Through Design**

A combination of storyline, interactivity, and sensory engagement is required to create engaging VR and AR experiences:

- **Storytelling**: Create a backstory or setting that engrosses readers in the action. A compelling plot can increase interest and foster strong feelings.

- **Interactivity:** Include interactive components that let users change the surroundings and results. This includes interactive characters, manipulable objects, and dynamic surroundings that react to user input.

- **Sensory Engagement:** To improve immersion, make use of tactile, aural, and visual feedback. A more realistic experience is enhanced by tactile feedback devices, spatial audio, and high-quality images.

## 5. VR and AR UI/UX Design

User engagement and pleasure are contingent upon the effective design of the user interface (UI) and user experience (UX).

- **Intuitive Navigation:** Create user-friendly, intuitive navigation solutions. This could incorporate hand tracking or gaze-based interactions in VR, and touch-based interactions in AR.

- **Consistency:** Retain uniformity in feedback, interactions, and visual design. Consistent design cues ease consumers' discomfort and lighten their cognitive strain.

- **Accessibility:** Make sure users of different abilities can utilise the application. This includes functions like text size adjustments, voice commands, and many input options.

## 6. Optimisation of Performance

Delivering seamless and responsive experiences requires performance optimisation, particularly in VR and AR applications:

- **Efficient Asset Management:** To lessen the computational burden, optimise 3D models, textures, and animations. Employ strategies such as level of detail (LOD) to efficiently allocate resources.

- **Rendering Techniques:** To increase performance, use sophisticated rendering techniques like baked lighting, occlusion culling, and frustum culling.

- **Latency Reduction:** Reduce latency to guarantee real-time interaction (Latency Reduction). Input handling, frame rates, and network connection must all be optimised for this.

## 7. Examination and Repetition

The development of VR and AR applications requires constant testing and iteration.

- **User Testing:** To get input and find usability problems, do frequent user testing. Surveys, focus groups, and beta testing are a few examples of this.

- **Performance Testing:** Verify the application's performance and stability under a range of circumstances. Compatibility, load, and stress testing are all included in this.

- **Iteration:** Make iterative improvements to the application based on user feedback and test findings. This procedure can be streamlined with the use of agile development approaches.

## 8. Privacy and Security

In VR and AR applications, where users interact with sensitive data and digital assets, security and privacy are crucial.

- **Data Protection:** To safeguard user data and transactions, put strong encryption and data protection procedures in place.

- **User Authentication:** To improve security, use secure login procedures and multi-factor authentication.

- **Privacy Policies:** Provide consumers with control over their data and establish explicit privacy policies. Openness on the gathering and application of data fosters trust.

## 9. Strategies for Monetization

Depending on the type of application, monetization tactics for VR and AR applications can differ significantly:

- **In-App Purchases:** Charge for in-app virtual items, upgrades, and personalisation choices.

- **Subscription Models:** Provide access to premium features, material, or services through a subscription model.

- **Advertising:** Incorporate discreet advertising into the online space. This can include virtual billboards, sponsored events, and branded areas.

The creation of VR and AR applications is a thrilling and difficult task that calls for a fusion of creative design, technical know-how, and user-centered thinking. Developers may create engrossing and captivating virtual and augmented realities by utilising key technology, selecting appropriate development platforms, and concentrating on immersive experiences. The likelihood of success is further increased by paying attention to UI/UX design, performance optimisation, security, and monetization techniques. There are countless prospects for creative and significant applications of VR and AR technologies as they develop, providing new means for people to engage, educate, and amuse themselves in virtual spaces.

## ➢ Blockchain and NFT Integration in the Metaverse

Non-fungible tokens (NFTs) and blockchain technology combined with the Metaverse mark a revolutionary transformation in the production, ownership, and trade of digital assets. These technologies create a transparent and decentralised framework that allows for digital ownership, safe and verifiable transactions, and innovative economic models in virtual environments. The foundations of blockchain and NFTs, their functions in the Metaverse, and useful tips for incorporating these technologies into Metaverse applications are all covered in this essay.

## 1. Gaining Knowledge on Blockchain Technology

Blockchain is a distributed ledger system that is decentralised and records transactions across several computers in a way that prevents records from being changed after the fact. Data security, transparency, and immutability are therefore guaranteed.

- **Decentralisation:** Since blockchain runs on a peer-to-peer network, a central authority is superseded.

- **Security:** Blockchain is extremely resistant to fraud and hacking thanks to cryptographic techniques that secure transactions.

- **Transparency:** All transactions are entered into a public ledger that is open to public auditing.

- **Immutability:** Transactions are unchangeable once they are recorded, protecting the accuracy of the data.

**2. Non-Fungible Tokens (NFTs)**

NFTs are distinct digital assets that have been blockchain-verified. NFTs are indivisible and unique, in contrast to cryptocurrencies like Bitcoin and Ethereum, which are fungible and may be traded one-to-one.

- **Uniqueness:** Every NFT is identified by a special code that sets it apart from other tokens.

- **Provenance:** For digital art and collectibles, NFTs offer a verifiable history of ownership and origin.

- **Interoperability:** NFTs are usable in a variety of Metaverse ecosystems and platforms.

## 3. The Metaverse's Use of Blockchain and NFTs

In the Metaverse, blockchain technology and NFTs facilitate new kinds of communication, ownership, and commerce, among other essential functions.

- **Digital Ownership:** Virtual property, avatars, and in-game goods are among the digital assets for which blockchain guarantees verifiable and secure ownership.

- **Interoperable Economies:** NFTs enable the development of digital economies that are interoperable and allow for the trading of assets between various Metaverse platforms.

- **Smart Contracts:** Self-executing contracts with conditions encoded directly into code, smart contracts automate and secure transactions. Blockchain technology makes them possible.

- **Decentralised Governance:** Users can take part in governance and decision-making procedures in decentralised autonomous organisations (DAOs), which are made possible by blockchain technology.

## 4. Achievable Integration Considerations

Careful planning and evaluation of numerous technical and user experience elements are necessary when integrating blockchain and NFTs into Metaverse apps.

### A. Selecting the Appropriate Blockchain

Applications for the Metaverse can be run on a number of blockchain platforms, each having pros and cons.

- **Ethereum:** Known for its strong ecosystem and smart contract capabilities, this blockchain is the most popular choice for NFTs. But it has problems with scalability and expensive transaction fees.

- **Flow:** Compared to Ethereum, this protocol offers faster transactions and lower transaction fees, making it ideal for high-throughput applications like gaming and NFTs.

- **Polygon (Matic):** An Ethereum layer-2 scaling solution that takes advantage of Ethereum's security to offer quicker and less expensive transactions.

- **Binance Smart Chain:** Less decentralised than Ethereum, yet it offers cheaper fees and quicker transaction times.

### B. Putting NFTs in Place

NFT creation and management require the following steps:

- **Minting:** The process of producing a unique token on the blockchain in order to create an NFT. Custom smart contracts or platforms such as OpenSea and Rarible can be used for this.

- **Storage:** To guarantee availability and immutability, decentralised storage solutions like IPFS (InterPlanetary File System) are frequently used to store the digital material connected with NFTs, such as pictures or 3D models.

- **Metadata:** Making certain that the NFT's name, description, and other pertinent information are safely kept and connected to the token.

**C. Safety and Observance**

It is critical to guarantee the security and legal compliance of blockchain and NFT implementations:

- **Smart Contract Audits:** To find and fix vulnerabilities, conduct routine smart contract audits.

- **Compliance with regulations:** Since rules and regulations pertaining to digital assets might differ depending on the jurisdiction, keep up with the latest developments in this area.

- **User Education:** Inform users about the hazards associated with blockchain transactions and best procedures for protecting their digital wallets.

## D. Improving the User Interface

The user experience should be improved by integrating blockchain and NFTs rather than made more difficult:

- **Seamless Wallet Integration:** Make NFT storage and transactions simple with wallet connectors. Popular options include Coinbase Wallet and MetaMask.

- **User-Friendly Interfaces:** Create simple-to-use interfaces for NFT trading, management, and minting. Simplifying complicated procedures will increase user adoption.

- **Cross-Platform Interoperability:** Make certain that digital assets and NFTs may be utilised with various Metaverse platforms and apps.

## 5. Applications and Use Cases

The combination of blockchain technology with NFTs opens up a wide range of creative applications in the Metaverse.

- **Virtual Real Estate:** Users can purchase, trade, and construct virtual land parcels protected by NFTs on websites like Decentraland and The Sandbox.

- **Digital Art and Collectibles:** Tokenizing their creations as NFTs opens up new revenue streams and guarantees provenance for artists and makers. This is made possible by platforms such as Foundation and Art Blocks.

- **Gaming:** NFTs are used to represent in-game assets in games like Axie Infinity and CryptoKitties, enabling players to exchange and profit from their virtual goods.

- **Identity and Avatars:** Users can take control of their identity and personalisation in the Metaverse by using blockchain to protect digital IDs and avatars.

- **Event Tickets and Access Control:** By serving as virtual event tickets, NFTs guarantee authenticity and thwart fraud.

A fundamental shift in the creation, ownership, and interaction of digital assets is presented by the integration of blockchain and NFTs into the Metaverse. Developers may create safe, transparent, and interoperable virtual worlds that empower users and open up new economic opportunities by utilising the distinctive qualities of these technologies. Blockchain and NFTs will play an increasingly important part in the Metaverse's growth and evolution, spurring innovation and changing the way people interact with digital platforms.

## ➢ Using Machine Learning and AI in the Metaverse

The Metaverse is a collective virtual shared place that has attracted a lot of attention from a variety of businesses. It is formed by combining digitally augmented physical reality with physically persistent virtual space. Artificial Intelligence (AI) and Machine Learning (ML) technologies have the potential to revolutionise user experiences, optimise processes, and generate novel avenues for innovation when they are integrated into the Metaverse. The foundations of AI and ML, their uses in the Metaverse, and the possible advantages and difficulties of utilising these technologies are all covered in this article.

### 1. Comprehend Artificial Intelligence and Machine Learning**

**Artificial Intelligence (AI):** AI is the term used to describe how computers, mostly computer systems, can simulate human intelligence processes. Learning, reasoning, problem-solving, perception, and language comprehension are some of these processes.

**Machine Learning (ML):** A branch of artificial intelligence, ML uses statistical models and algorithms to teach computers to carry out certain tasks without explicit instructions, instead relying on patterns and inference.

## 2. AI and ML Applications in the Metaverse

The Metaverse can be improved by applying AI and ML in a variety of ways to make it more interactive, efficient, and immersive.

### A. Improving The User Interface

**Personalisation:** AI systems are able to provide recommendations, experiences, and information that are tailored to each user's preferences and behaviour within the Metaverse. This comprises customised avatars, virtual worlds, and educational or recreational materials.

**Natural Language Processing (NLP):** NLP facilitates more intuitive and natural communication between users and non-player characters (NPCs) or virtual assistants. Among the apps that improve interaction and communication are voice recognition, sentiment analysis, and language translation.

**Realistic Avatars:** By evaluating user data, including images or videos, AI can produce 3D models that faithfully depict users in virtual environments, resulting in extremely realistic and expressive avatars. This improves the immersion and sense of presence.

**B. Content Creation Automation**

**Procedural Generation:** By generating large and varied virtual landscapes, buildings, and objects, AI-driven procedural generation can lessen the need for human content development. This allows the Metaverse to grow quickly without sacrificing its high levels of complexity and diversity.

**AI Art and Design:** AI tools can help with music compositions, artwork, and Metaverse design aspects. These tools promote creativity and innovation by producing original content or working with human producers to improve their work.

## C. Sensible NPCs and Agents

**Advanced NPCs:** NPCs with lifelike interactions and behaviours can be powered by AI and ML. These clever agents are able to create more dynamic and interesting experiences by responding to user actions and learning from them.

**Virtual Assistants:** Using information, direction, and support, AI-powered virtual assistants can assist users in navigating the Metaverse. By understanding and responding to voice commands, these assistants improve usability and accessibility.

## D. Examining and Interpreting Data

**User Behaviour Analysis:** Patterns, preferences, and trends can be found in user data by ML algorithms. Business choices, user engagement, and virtual environment optimisation can all be aided by this data.

**Predictive Analytics:** AI is able to anticipate user requirements and actions, which enables proactive support and customised interactions. This can involve proposing fresh initiatives, projecting virtual infrastructure maintenance requirements, or allocating resources as efficiently as possible.

## E. Moderating and Security

**Fraud Detection:** Artificial intelligence algorithms are capable of identifying security risks and fraudulent activity in the Metaverse, including unauthorised access, deception, and hostile conduct. This improves virtual spaces' integrity and safety.

**Content Moderation:** By monitoring and removing offensive or dangerous content, AI-powered moderation technologies can make sure that every user is in a secure and friendly environment. Hate speech, inflammatory language, and other transgressions of social norms can all be found with these methods.

## 3. Advantages of Using ML and AI in the Metaverse

There are numerous noteworthy advantages to the Metaverse's incorporation of AI and ML technology.

- **Enhanced Immersion:** More realistic avatars, intelligent NPCs, and AI-driven personalisation provide for more captivating and immersive experiences.

- **Scalability:** The Metaverse can be scaled more easily since AI and ML make it possible to quickly create and operate enormous virtual environments.

- **Efficiency:** By automating the generation and moderation of content, less manual involvement is required, which streamlines processes and lowers expenses.

- **Innovation:** The creation of new experiences and apps is made possible by AI-powered tools and insights that stimulate creativity and innovation.

- **Security:** Sophisticated AI algorithms improve moderation and security, resulting in virtual environments that are more trustworthy and safe.

### 4. Difficulties and Things to Think About

Although incorporating AI and ML into the Metaverse has many advantages, there are a number of drawbacks as well:

**Data Privacy:** Concerns about privacy are raised by the gathering and analysis of user data. Enforcing applicable legislation and putting strong data protection procedures in place are essential.

**Bias and Fairness:** Prejudices that exist in the training data may unintentionally be reinforced by AI systems. These algorithms must be continuously monitored and adjusted to ensure inclusion and fairness.

**Technical Complexity:** A large amount of technical know-how and resources are required to develop and implement AI and ML solutions in the Metaverse. For smaller developers or organisations, this might be a hindrance.

**Ethical Considerations:** Concerns around user autonomy, consent, and manipulation are brought up by the application of AI in the Metaverse. In order to address these concerns, precise norms and ethical standards are required.

**Interoperability:** A coherent experience depends on AI and ML systems' ability to integrate with different platforms and technologies within the Metaverse.

The Metaverse could be completely changed by AI and ML technologies, leading to the creation of more efficient, engaging, and immersive virtual worlds. Developers may improve user experiences, create content automatically, and maintain security and moderation by utilising these technologies. To integrate AI and ML into the Metaverse responsibly and ethically, however, means tackling the related issues of data privacy, bias, and technical complexity. These technologies will surely be crucial in determining how digital interactions and virtual experiences develop in the future as they continue to advance.

# Chapter Five

# The Metaverse Economy

The way we engage with digital surroundings is being revolutionised by the Metaverse, a collective virtual shared place that includes virtual reality (VR), augmented reality (AR), and the Internet. This emerging digital world is changing entertainment and social connections, but it's also bringing forth a whole new economic environment. This article examines the Metaverse's underlying economic theories, developing economic models, the function of digital assets, and the opportunities and problems it brings.

## 1. The Metaverse's Basic Economic Principles

With certain digital quirks, the economics of the Metaverse are regulated by laws akin to those of the real world.

**Supply and Demand:** The Metaverse's digital products

and services are governed by the fundamental law of supply and demand. The scarcity, usefulness, and desirability of virtual land, digital art, and in-game objects determine their respective values.

**Value Creation:** In the Metaverse, value is generated by user interaction, inventiveness, and creativity. Value is created by participants, developers, and content creators who add to the diversity and richness of the virtual environment.

**Exchange Mechanisms:** Digital currencies, namely cryptocurrencies, and blockchain technology enable transactions inside the Metaverse, guaranteeing safe, open, and effective exchanges.

### 2. New Approaches to Economics

A number of cutting-edge economic models are introduced by the Metaverse, which redefines conventional corporate procedures and revenue-generating strategies.

## A. Digital Property

- **Virtual Land Ownership:** Owning virtual land in the Metaverse has grown to be a profitable venture, just like in the real world. Users can buy, create, and profit from virtual real estate through platforms such as Decentraland and The Sandbox.

- **Leasing and Renting:** Virtual landowners can make passive revenue by leasing or renting their digital properties for a variety of uses, like holding events, establishing virtual stores, or developing immersive experiences.

## B. Electronic Products and Services

- **NFT Marketplaces:** Non-fungible tokens, or NFTs, facilitate the production and exchange of one-of-a-kind digital goods, such as virtual clothing, music, art, and collectibles. These transactions are made possible by NFT markets like OpenSea and Rarible, which bolster the thriving digital economy.

- **In-Game Economies:** A lot of Metaverse platforms have complex in-game economies that allow users to exchange, earn, and spend virtual assets and currencies. Axie Infinity and Fortnite are two examples of games with strong in-game economies that encourage player engagement and inventiveness.

## C. Economy Driven by Social and Community Factors

- **Decentralised Autonomous Organisations (DAOs):** These are community-driven organisations with decentralised governance in which interested parties collaborate to make choices. DAOs have the ability to fund projects, oversee virtual environments, and produce wealth through cooperation in the Metaverse.

- **Social Tokens:** Digital assets that signify possession or community membership are called social tokens. These tokens can be redeemed for rewards to the community, voting privileges, and access to special material.

### D. Producing and Profiting from Content

- **Creator Economies:** Direct sales, subscriptions, and microtransactions are three ways that content creators can make money from their creations. Creators are supported by platforms such as Substack and Patreon, which help artists grow and make money from their audiences.

- **Sponsorships and Advertising:** To reach interested audiences, brands can use influencer relationships, branded experiences, and virtual billboards to sponsor and advertise events inside the Metaverse.

### 3. Digital Assets' Role

The Metaverse's economic structure revolves around digital assets, which include virtual goods, NFTs, and cryptocurrencies.

- **Cryptocurrencies:** In the Metaverse, cryptocurrencies like Bitcoin, Ethereum, and tokens unique to a particular platform (like MANA for Decentraland) allow for value storage and transactional support. They offer a decentralised, international medium of trade.

- **NFTs:** NFTs guarantee provenance and scarcity by representing ownership of distinct digital goods. They are used to exchange virtual real estate, artwork, collectibles, and other items, opening up new markets for investors and artists.

- **Virtual Goods:** In the Metaverse, virtual goods such as avatars, skins, accessories, and products improve user experiences and allow for more self-expression. Their rarity, usefulness, and beauty determine their value.

### 4. Difficulties and Possibilities

The Metaverse offers tremendous economic potential, but there are also a number of serious problems that must be resolved.

## A. Difficulties

- **Regulatory Uncertainty:** The rules governing virtual economies and digital assets are still changing. To guarantee legal compliance, safeguard customers, and promote innovation, precise criteria are required.

- **Digital Divide**: Affordability and technological infrastructure restrict access to the Metaverse. It is imperative to guarantee inclusion and equitable chances for every user.

- **Privacy and Security:** Because the Metaverse is decentralised, there are security issues to be aware of, such as fraud, hacking, and data breaches. To keep users safe, strong security protocols and privacy safeguards are necessary.

- **Economic Stability:** The Metaverse may experience economic instability as a result of the volatility of cryptocurrencies and other digital assets. Inflation control and value stability mechanisms are required.

## B. Possibilities

**- invention and Creativity:** New forms of expression, entertainment, and business ventures are made possible by the Metaverse's atmosphere of unrestricted creativity and invention.

**- New Marketplaces:** The Metaverse expands the potential available to creators, entrepreneurs, and enterprises by generating new markets for digital goods and services.

**- Global Connectivity:** The Metaverse allows for worldwide cooperation, trade, and social contact by overcoming geographic barriers.

**- Economic Empowerment:** People and groups are empowered to shape and direct their own economic destinies due to the decentralised structure of the Metaverse.

Conventional ideas of value, ownership, and trade are

being transformed by the economics of the Metaverse. The Metaverse presents unparalleled prospects for innovation, entrepreneurship, and economic expansion through the use of decentralised technologies, creative digital assets, and inventive economic structures. But to fully realise the potential of this new digital economy, issues with stability, security, access, and regulation must be resolved. The Metaverse will surely have a revolutionary impact on how people connect digitally and conduct business in the future as it develops further.

## ➤ Digital Assets and Virtual Economies

The Metaverse, a linked network of augmented and virtual reality spaces, is pushing the boundaries of digital commerce. Virtual economies and digital assets, which allow users to purchase, sell, and exchange products and services in immersive settings, are at the centre of this transition. In the digital age, these factors are changing the ways that value is created, traded, and understood.

## 1. Digital Marketplaces

Within the boundaries of the Metaverse, virtual economies function in a manner similar to that of traditional economies but with distinctive digital twists.

**In-Game Economies****:** Virtual worlds with strong economies, like those in online games like "World of Warcraft" or "Second Life," allow players to make, spend, and exchange virtual currency. User interactions, such as exchanging commodities, doing tasks, and taking part in events, power these economies.

**Marketplace Platforms:** Decentraland and The Sandbox are two examples of platforms that provide virtual assets and land for purchase and development. These platforms establish virtual communities where users may develop, exchange, and profit from their works of art.

**Social Economies:** Using social tokens, which stand for influence and membership in a group, communities in the Metaverse can create their own economic structures. Voting, gaining access to premium content, and rewarding contributions are all possible using these tokens.

## 2. Digital Assets

The fundamental units of virtual economies are digital assets, which include anything from exclusive digital goods to virtual real estate.

- **Cryptocurrencies:** The main form of money in the Metaverse is cryptocurrency, such as Bitcoin and Ethereum. In addition to storing wealth and facilitating transactions, they offer a decentralised, international financial infrastructure.

- **Non-Fungible Tokens (NFTs):** NFTs are distinct digital tokens that stand in for ownership of particular property, including virtual land, artwork, collectibles, and in-game goods. They offer real and verifiable proof of ownership, creating scarcity and demand that drives value.

- **Virtual Goods:** things that may be bought, traded, and used in virtual settings include avatars, skins, accessories, and other in-game things. Their uniqueness, usefulness, and visual appeal are frequently what make them valuable.

➢ **Strategies for Monetization and Business Models**

Businesses have more options to produce and capture value as the Metaverse expands. There are a growing number of business models and monetization techniques that enable organisations and people to make money from their virtual activities.

## 1. Direct Sales

**- Digital products:** One simple way to make money is to sell people virtual products directly. This might range from customised NFTs to virtual apparel for avatars.

**- Virtual Real Estate:** It is possible to purchase, develop, and sell virtual real estate for a profit, just like in the real world. Virtual stores, galleries, and experiences that draw customers and bring in money can be made by owners.

## 2. Subscription Services

**- Premium Access:** Providing premium experiences or content via subscription services is a typical business strategy. To gain access to premium regions, services, or material in the Metaverse, users must pay a regular price.

- **Membership Programmes:** DAOs and social tokens can support membership schemes in which users can sign up to gain access to special material, vote in decisions, and earn benefits.

## 3. Sponsorships and Advertising

- **Virtual Advertising:** Sponsored events, branded content, and virtual billboards are some of the ways that brands can advertise in the Metaverse. This raises brand awareness in a new digital space in addition to producing income.

- **Influencer Partnerships:** Collaborating with well-known online influencers or content producers to market goods and services can be a very successful strategy. Brands can use these influencers' devoted fan bases to further their marketing campaigns.

## 4. Earn by Playing Models

- **In-Game Earnings:** By playing games, players can

earn digital assets or cryptocurrencies through play-to-earn methods. Players can make money off of these gains by trading or selling them.

- **Staking and Yield Farming:** Similar to conventional investing techniques in decentralised finance (DeFi), users can stake their digital assets or take part in yield farming in blockchain-based Metaverse platforms to gain rewards.

5. Token Sales and Crowdfunding

- **Initial Coin Offerings (ICOs):** Businesses can launch an ICO to raise capital by issuing tokens of their own. These tokens can be used inside the Metaverse, to represent ownership stakes, or to gain access to services.

- **Crowdfunding Campaigns:** Through the use of crowdfunding systems, projects in the Metaverse can raise money from the public while providing backers with exclusive benefits or first access to material.

## ➢ Case Studies of Profitable Metaverse Efforts

Analysing profitable endeavours in the Metaverse offers important insights into the possibilities and best practices of this new business environment.

### 1. Decentraland

**Overview:** Based on the Ethereum blockchain, Decentraland is a decentralised virtual environment. Virtual land can be bought, developed, and made profitable by users.

**Success Factors:** Decentraland's decentralised governance mechanism, lively community, and strong virtual asset market are its key success factors. Both a sizable user base and substantial investment have been drawn to the platform.

**Revenue Streams:** Land sales, transaction fees, and alliances with developers and brands are how

Decentraland makes money.

**2. Infinity Axie**

**Overview:** Players can gather, breed, and engage in combat with Axies, fantastical animals, in the blockchain-based game Axie Infinity. It uses a play-to-earn business model, giving players cryptocurrency in exchange for their in-game actions.

**Success Factors:** The game's robust community, interesting gameplay, and abundant earning potential have all helped to fuel its appeal. Many gamers now rely heavily on Axie Infinity for their money, especially those who live in developing nations.

**Revenue Streams:** In-game purchases, marketplace commissions, and the selling of Axies and other digital goods are how Axie Infinity makes money.

**3. The Sandbox**

**Overview:** Users may develop, own, and profit from their game experiences in the Sandbox, a virtual universe. To guarantee digital asset ownership and scarcity, it makes use of blockchain technology.

**Success Factors:** The Sandbox's success has been fueled by its emphasis on user-generated content, collaborations with well-known brands, and a thriving developer and creator community.

**Revenue Streams:** Land sales, transaction fees, and partnerships with companies and content producers are how the platform makes money.

Traditional economic structures are being altered by the Metaverse, which is also opening up new avenues for value creation and commercialization. At the centre of this change are virtual economies and digital assets, which open up new revenue sources and business models. Businesses and individuals can prosper in the dynamic and quickly changing Metaverse world by comprehending and utilising these components. Entrepreneurs seeking to traverse and profit from this digital frontier can learn a lot from successful projects like Decentraland, Axie Infinity, and The Sandbox.

## Chapter Six

## Social and Ethical Factors in the Development of the Metaverse

The growth and development of the Metaverse, a communal virtual shared space that combines the Internet, virtual reality (VR), and augmented reality (AR), holds the potential to revolutionise a variety of fields, including social interactions and economics. These opportunities do, however, bring with them important social and ethical issues that need to be addressed by developers, users, legislators, and society at general. These factors are examined in this article together with privacy, security, inclusivity, and possible psychological effects of prolonged virtual participation.

### 1. Concerns About Privacy

Particular privacy challenges arise from the massive volume of data generated by users and the immersive aspect of the Metaverse.

**Data Collection and Usage:** In order for virtual environments to work properly, a lot of data must be collected. This includes biometric data, location data, and user behaviour patterns. It is crucial to make sure that this data is gathered, kept, and used appropriately.

**Consent and Transparency:** Users need to be made completely aware of the types of data being gathered and how they will be utilised. Building trust and ensuring ethical data practices require clear consent procedures and transparent data policies.

**Surveillance and Tracking:** There are serious ethical questions raised by the possibility of tracking and surveillance in the Metaverse. A crucial difficulty is striking a balance between user safety and security requirements and respect for privacy.

## 2. Protective Concerns

The safeguarding of digital assets, user identities, and the integrity of virtual environments are all aspects of the complex problem of security in the metaverse.

**Cybersecurity:** A number of cyberthreats, including as fraud, identity theft, and hacking, can affect the Metaverse. Strong cybersecurity defences are necessary to safeguard users' digital assets.

**Digital Identity Theft:** As users spend more time in the Metaverse, criminals are more interested in stealing their digital identities. It is essential to guarantee safe authentication procedures and safeguard personal data.

**Content Moderation:** It can be difficult to control user-generated content in order to stop harassment, hate speech, and other negative actions. In order to keep virtual environments inclusive and safe, effective moderating methods and regulations are required.

## 3. Accessibility and Inclusion

The Metaverse holds immense promise as a means of promoting social cohesion, education, and job possibilities for people worldwide. But it's imperative to guarantee accessibility and inclusivity.

**Digital Divide:** Many people, especially in underdeveloped areas, may not have access to modern technology and internet connectivity, which is necessary to access the Metaverse. It is imperative to close the digital gap in order to provide equitable opportunities for everybody.

**Diversity and Representation:** It is imperative to guarantee that the Metaverse is inclusive and accurately reflects a range of identities, ethnicities, and backgrounds. It is the responsibility of developers to make environments that both foster inclusion and reflect the diversity of humankind.

**Accessibility for Disabled people:** It is imperative that the Metaverse be made accessible to people with disabilities by providing accommodations. This entails making sure assistive devices are available and creating user interfaces and experiences that are accessible to a broad variety of abilities.

### 4. Social and Psychological Effects

Users who spend a lot of time in virtual environments may experience substantial social and psychological effects.

- **Mental Health:** Although the Metaverse can offer chances for amusement and social contact, it can also exacerbate mental health conditions including depression, addiction, and social isolation. It's critical to keep an eye on and treat the psychological effects of Metaverse use.

- **Identity and Self-Perception:** Users' sense of reality and self-perception may be impacted by their capacity to construct and maintain virtual identities. Mental health depends on maintaining a balance between one's virtual and real-world identities and experiences.

- **Social Dynamics:** The formation and maintenance of relationships are among the social dynamics that the Metaverse can change. It's critical to comprehend these shifts and encourage constructive social interactions in virtual worlds.

## 5. Design and Development Ethics

Adhering to user-centric design principles and taking into account potential societal implications are necessary for developing the Metaverse in an ethical manner.

**User Agency and Control:** A key component of ethical design is guaranteeing that users have authority over their virtual experiences, including the capacity to manage their data, personalise their settings, and establish boundaries.

**Ethical AI and Automation:** Bias, justice, and responsibility are some of the ethical issues that arise from the application of artificial intelligence (AI) in the Metaverse. It is crucial to make sure AI systems are developed and used ethically.

**Sustainability:** The Metaverse's creation and upkeep demand a large amount of processing power, which raises questions about the sustainability of the environment. Developers need to think about how their technology will affect the environment and work towards sustainable practices.

### 6. Regulatory and Legal Aspects

The Metaverse's legal and regulatory environment is still developing, with important ramifications for user rights, security, and privacy.

**Regulatory Frameworks:** To safeguard users and

guarantee equitable behaviours, it is imperative to establish explicit regulatory frameworks to oversee the Metaverse. This covers laws pertaining to virtual commerce, digital assets, and data protection.

**Intellectual Property:** Safeguarding the rights to digital works and virtual products in the Metaverse is a complicated matter. To protect the rights of creators, precise regulations and means for enforcement are required.

**Jurisdictional Challenges:** The worldwide reach of the Metaverse poses jurisdictional issues, especially with regard to regulation and enforcement. To properly handle these concerns, harmonisation of laws and international collaboration are needed.

Many social and ethical issues are raised by the Metaverse's development, and they must be carefully considered in order to guarantee that everyone will benefit from, be safe on, and enjoy this new digital frontier. Inclusion, security, privacy, and mental health are important issues that call for constant care and preventative action. Stakeholders may help form a Metaverse that not only improves digital experiences but also preserves the values and rights of its users by adopting ethical design principles, encouraging inclusivity, and establishing clear regulatory frameworks.

## ➢ Security and Privacy Issues

The merger of virtually improved physical reality and physically persistent virtual reality has generated the Metaverse, a collective virtual shared place that is rapidly developing. This development brings with it tremendous social and ethical concerns in addition to intriguing prospects. Driven by technologies like blockchain, AI, VR, AR, and IoT, this digital frontier has the potential to revolutionise a number of industries. To maintain a positive and inclusive Metaverse, however, the complications of privacy, security, legal frameworks, and ethical interactions must be properly addressed. This article explores three important topics: the ethical ramifications of Metaverse interaction, regulatory and legal issues, and privacy and security problems.

**1. Concerns About Privacy**

Because the Metaverse is so immersive, a large quantity of user data must be collected and processed, which raises serious privacy concerns.

**- Data Collection and Usage:** In order for virtual environments to operate efficiently, a lot of data is collected. This includes location data, behavioural patterns, and biometric information. Protecting user privacy requires taking great care to ensure that this data is gathered, preserved, and utilised properly.

**- Informed Consent and Transparency:** Users need to be made fully aware of the purpose of the data collection as well as its intended usage. Establishing ethical data practices and fostering trust require clear consent procedures and transparent data policies.

- **Surveillance and Tracking:** A significant ethical worry is the possibility of widespread tracking and surveillance within the Metaverse. It's crucial to strike a balance between user safety and security requirements and respect for the private.

## 2. Protective Concerns

Protecting digital assets, user identities, and the integrity of virtual environments are all included in the concept of security in the Metaverse.

- **Cybersecurity:** A number of cyberthreats, including fraud, identity theft, and hacking, can affect the Metaverse. Strong cybersecurity defences are necessary to keep hackers away from users' digital assets.

- **Digital Identity Theft:** Users' digital identities become valuable targets as they spend more time in the Metaverse. It is essential to protect personal information and use secure authentication techniques in order to stop identity theft.

- **Content Moderation:** To stop harassment, hate speech, and other negative activities, user-generated content must be effectively moderated. To keep safe and welcoming virtual environments, comprehensive moderation tools and policies must be put into place.

➢ **Legal and Regulatory Difficulties**

Because the Metaverse is decentralised and global, there are a lot of legal and regulatory issues that need to be resolved in order to protect users and maintain fair practices.

**1. Legal Structures**

Clear regulatory frameworks must be established in order to control the Metaverse and safeguard user rights.

- **Data Protection Laws:** Rules for user privacy and data protection are provided by laws like the CCPA and GDPR. Ensuring ethical data practices in the Metaverse requires the application of these frameworks.

**- Digital Asset Regulation:** To stop fraud, money laundering, and other financial crimes, extensive regulatory oversight is necessary given the growth of digital assets and cryptocurrencies in the Metaverse.

## 2. Property of the Intellectual

The digital and easily replicable nature of virtual creations makes IP rights protection in the Metaverse challenging.

**- IP Enforcement:** To protect creators' rights and stop IP theft, clear policies and enforcement procedures are required.

**- NFTs and Ownership:** There are concerns regarding the enforceability and legal standing of claims made regarding ownership of digital assets when non-fungible tokens (NFTs) are used to represent ownership.

### 3. Difficulties with Jurisdiction

The Metaverse's global scope makes jurisdictional concerns more difficult, especially when it comes to regulation and legal enforcement.

- **Cross-Border Regulations:** International collaboration and harmonization of legislation are needed to address jurisdictional difficulties efficiently.

- **Legal Accountability:** Determining legal accountability and liability within the Metaverse is complex, requiring clear legal frameworks and international agreements.

## ➢ Ethical Implications of Metaverse Interaction

The ethical implications of Metaverse interactions encompass various aspects, including inclusivity, mental well-being, and responsible design.

## 1. Inclusivity and Accessibility

Ensuring that the Metaverse is inclusive and accessible to all individuals, regardless of their background or abilities, is critical.

- **Digital Divide:** Access to advanced technology and internet connectivity is necessary to participate in the Metaverse. It is imperative to close the digital gap in order to provide equitable opportunities for everybody.

- **Diversity and Representation:** Creating environments that reflect diverse cultures, backgrounds, and identities promotes inclusivity and enriches the Metaverse experience.

- **Accessibility for Disabled Users:** Designing interfaces and experiences that are usable by people with disabilities is crucial to ensure accessibility and inclusivity.

## 2. Mental Health and Well-Being

Extended engagement with virtual environments can have significant psychological impacts on users.

- **Mental Health:** Although the Metaverse can offer chances for amusement and social contact, it can also exacerbate mental health conditions including depression, addiction, and social isolation. Monitoring and addressing these impacts is essential.

- **Identity and Self-Perception:** Users' sense of reality and self-perception may be impacted by their capacity to construct and maintain virtual identities. Mental health depends on maintaining a balance between one's virtual and real-world identities and experiences.

- **Social Dynamics:** Understanding the changes in social dynamics brought about by the Metaverse and promoting positive interactions is important for fostering a healthy virtual society.

## 3. Ethical Design and Development

Adhering to user-centric design principles and taking into account potential societal implications are necessary for developing the Metaverse in an ethical manner.

- **User Agency and Control:** Ensuring that users have control over their virtual experiences, including data management and customization options, is fundamental to ethical design.

- **Ethical AI and Automation:** Bias, justice, and responsibility are some of the ethical issues that arise from the application of artificial intelligence (AI) in the Metaverse. It is crucial to make sure AI systems are developed and used ethically.

- **Sustainability:** The Metaverse's creation and upkeep demand a large amount of processing power, which raises questions about the sustainability of the environment. Developers need to think about how their technology will affect the environment and work towards sustainable practices.

Many social and ethical issues are raised by the Metaverse's development, and they must be carefully considered in order to guarantee that everyone will benefit from, be safe on, and enjoy this new digital frontier. Privacy, security, inclusivity, mental well-being, and ethical design are critical areas that require ongoing attention and proactive measures. By embracing ethical design principles, fostering inclusivity, and establishing clear regulatory frameworks, stakeholders can help shape a Metaverse that enhances digital experiences while upholding the values and rights of its users.

# Chapter Seven

# Case Studies and Practical Illustrations in the Development of the Metaverse

The Metaverse's quick development has sparked a number of real-world applications in a variety of sectors, including gaming, social media, healthcare, and education. These case studies highlight the opportunities and difficulties pioneers in this digital frontier faced, while also illuminating the metaverse's transformative potential. In this article, we explore several notable examples of Metaverse applications, examining their impacts, successes, and the lessons learned.

## 1. Gaming and Social Interaction

**Fortnite by Epic Games**
**Overview:** Fortnite, a popular online game developed by Epic Games, has evolved into a social platform where players can interact, attend virtual events, and create

content.

**Impact:**

- **Social Hub:** Beyond its gaming roots, Fortnite has become a social space where millions gather for virtual events such as concerts, movie screenings, and live performances. Notable events include the Travis Scott concert, which drew over 12 million concurrent viewers.

- **User-Generated Content:** The game's Creative Mode allows players to design their own islands and game modes, fostering a vibrant community of creators.

**Challenges:**

- **Moderation:** Managing user-generated content and ensuring a safe environment for all players is an ongoing challenge.

- **Technical Constraints:** Hosting large-scale events requires significant technical infrastructure to ensure a seamless experience.

**Lessons Learned:**

- **Engagement through Events:** Hosting unique and engaging virtual events can drive user engagement and retention.
- **Community Involvement:** Empowering users to create and share content fosters a strong sense of community and innovation.

**Decentraland**

**Overview:** Decentraland is a decentralized virtual world built on the Ethereum blockchain, where users can buy, sell, and develop virtual real estate, participate in events, and create content.

**Impact:**

- **Digital Ownership:** Users own parcels of virtual land as NFTs, giving them true ownership and control over their digital assets.

- **Virtual Economy:** Decentraland has a thriving virtual economy, with users buying and selling land, goods, and services using the platform's cryptocurrency, MANA.

**Challenges:**

- **Scalability:** Blockchain technology, while secure, can face scalability issues, affecting transaction speeds and costs.

- **User Adoption:** Attracting and retaining users in a decentralized virtual world requires continuous innovation and community engagement.

**Lessons Learned:**

- **Empowering Users with Ownership:** Providing true digital ownership through blockchain technology can enhance user engagement and investment in the platform.

- **Building a Robust Economy:** A thriving virtual economy requires a well-designed system for transactions, trade, and value creation.

## 2. Healthcare and Therapy

**Virtual Reality Therapy**

**Overview:** Virtual reality (VR) is being used to provide therapeutic interventions for mental health issues, including anxiety, PTSD, and phobias.

**Impact:**

- **Immersive Therapy:** VR allows patients to confront and manage their conditions in a controlled, immersive environment. For example, VR therapy has been used effectively to treat PTSD in veterans by simulating combat scenarios.

- **Accessibility:** Virtual reality therapy is a useful tool for patients who might not have easy access to traditional therapy because it can be accessed remotely.

**Challenges:**

- **Accessibility and Cost:** High-quality VR equipment can be expensive, limiting accessibility for some patients.

- **Standardization:** Developing standardized protocols and ensuring the effectiveness of VR therapy across different conditions and populations is necessary.

**Lessons Learned:**

**- Effectiveness of Immersion:** The immersive nature of VR can significantly enhance therapeutic outcomes for various mental health conditions.

**- Remote Accessibility:** VR therapy offers a scalable solution to reach patients in remote or underserved areas.

## 3. Information and Instruction

**Engage VR Platform**
**Overview:** Engage is a virtual reality platform designed for education and corporate training, allowing users to create and participate in immersive learning experiences.

**Impact:**

**- Interactive Learning:** Engage provides interactive, immersive learning experiences that can enhance engagement and retention compared to traditional methods.

- **Global Reach:** The platform enables educators to reach students worldwide, breaking down geographical barriers to education.

**Challenges:**

- **Content Creation:** Developing high-quality, engaging VR educational content requires significant resources and expertise.

- **Technical Barriers:** Ensuring that all users have access to the requisite VR hardware and software can be a difficulty.

**Lessons Learned:**

- **Immersive Learning:** Immersive VR experiences can significantly enhance the effectiveness of educational and training programs.

- **Global Accessibility:** VR platforms can democratize access to education by connecting students and educators from around the world.

## 4. Virtual Reality in Medical Training

**Overview:** VR is increasingly used in medical training, providing a safe, controlled environment for practicing procedures and simulations.

**Impact:**

- **Simulation Training:** VR allows medical students and professionals to practice surgeries, emergency responses, and other procedures without risk to patients.

- **Skill Development:** VR training can improve procedural skills, decision-making, and confidence among medical professionals.

**Challenges:**

- **High Costs:** Developing and maintaining high-quality VR training programs can be costly.

- **Integration:** Integrating VR training into existing medical education programs requires careful planning and support.

**Lessons Learned:**

- **Safe Training Environments:** VR provides a safe, risk-free environment for medical training, enhancing skill development and confidence.

- **Enhanced Learning Outcomes:** VR training can improve learning outcomes by providing realistic, hands-on experiences that are difficult to replicate in traditional settings.

These case studies and real-world examples highlight the diverse applications and transformative potential of the

Metaverse across various industries. While the opportunities are vast, the challenges are equally significant, requiring continuous innovation, investment, and ethical considerations. The lessons learned from these pioneering efforts can guide future developments, ensuring that the Metaverse evolves into a beneficial and inclusive digital frontier for all. By understanding the successes and pitfalls of early Metaverse applications, stakeholders can build more robust, secure, and engaging virtual environments that enhance our digital experiences.

## ➢ Examining Current Metaverse Platforms

Techies, companies, and consumers all find themselves drawn to the Metaverse, a communal virtual shared environment made possible by the combination of persistent virtual worlds and virtually enhanced physical reality. This immersive digital ecosystem is being developed on a number of platforms, each with their own special qualities, advantages, and disadvantages. This analysis looks at a number of well-known Metaverse platforms, assessing their user bases, economic models, and technological underpinnings as well as the wider implications for virtual worlds in the future.

## 1. Life Beyond

One of the first and best-known virtual worlds, Second Life was introduced by Linden Lab in 2003 and provides a deep and engaging social environment.

**Technological Foundation:**
- **Graphics and Environment:** Avatars, objects, and landscapes can all be greatly customised in Second Life's 3D environment. Comparing its graphics to those of more recent platforms, they are a little dated.

- **Scripting Language:** Users can create intricate interactive objects and environments using the platform's proprietary scripting language, Linden Scripting Language (LSL).

**Experience for Users:**

**- Social and Community Network:** Second Life is well known for its active social network, which hosts events, groups, and in-world activities.

**- Customisation:** A strong sense of identity and ownership is fostered by the users' great freedom to personalise their avatars and create distinctive virtual spaces.

**Economic Model:**

**- Virtual Economy:** The Linden Dollar (L$), the currency of Second Life, is the foundation of a thriving virtual economy that can be exchanged for real money. Virtual goods and services can be purchased, sold, and traded by users.

**- Marketplaces:** The platform facilitates the purchase of land, apparel, accessories, and other digital goods by users through virtual marketplaces.

**Difficulties:**

- **User Base:** Compared to more recent platforms, Second Life's user base has stagnated, despite still being active.

- **Technical Limitations:** Attracting new users may be hampered by the platform's outdated interface and technology.

## 2. Decentraland

Decentraland is a decentralized virtual world built on the Ethereum blockchain, emphasizing user ownership and decentralized governance.

**Technological Foundation:**

- **Blockchain Integration:** Decentraland leverages blockchain technology to enable true ownership of digital assets through non-fungible tokens (NFTs). Land and other assets are represented as NFTs, providing verifiable ownership.

- **Virtual Reality:** While Decentraland is accessible through web browsers, it also supports VR headsets for a more immersive experience.

**User Experience:**

- **User-Created Content:** Users can create, explore, and trade virtual experiences and assets. The platform provides tools for building 3D environments and interactive applications.

- **Governance:** Decentraland features a decentralized autonomous organization (DAO) that allows users to participate in the decision-making process, shaping the platform's future development.

**Economic Model:**

- **Cryptocurrency:** The platform uses its native cryptocurrency, MANA, for transactions. Users can earn MANA through various activities and trade it on external cryptocurrency exchanges.

- **Virtual Land Market:** Land in Decentraland is a valuable asset, with parcels bought, sold, and developed by users. The virtual real estate market is a significant component of the platform's economy.

**Challenges:**
- **Scalability:** Blockchain-based platforms face scalability issues, including transaction speed and costs.

- **Adoption:** Attracting and retaining a big user base is vital for supporting the platform's business and community.

### 3. Roblox

Roblox is a massively popular online platform that allows users to create and play games created by other users, fostering a dynamic and creative community.

**Technological Foundation:**
- **Game Creation Tools:** Roblox provides an intuitive set of tools for game development, including a scripting language based on Lua. Users can create complex games

and interactive experiences without extensive programming knowledge.

- **Cross-Platform:** Roblox is accessible on multiple platforms, including PC, mobile devices, and gaming consoles, making it highly accessible.

**User Experience:**
- **Community and Social Features:** Roblox emphasizes social interaction, with features such as friends lists, chat, and collaborative game development.

- **User-Generated Content:** The platform thrives on user-generated content, with millions of games and experiences available. This diversity keeps the platform engaging and constantly evolving.

**Economic Model:**
- **Robux Currency:** Roblox uses a virtual currency called Robux, which can be purchased with real money or earned through game creation. Developers can monetize their games by selling in-game items and

features.

- **Developer Revenue:** Successful developers can earn significant income, with Roblox sharing a portion of the revenue generated from their games.

**Challenges:**

- **Content Moderation:** With a vast amount of user-generated content, ensuring a safe and appropriate environment for all users, especially younger ones, is a significant challenge.

- **Revenue Sharing:** Some developers and users have criticized the revenue-sharing model, arguing that it favors the platform over individual creators.

### 4. VRChat

VRChat is a social VR platform that allows users to interact in a variety of virtual worlds using custom avatars.

**Technological Foundation:**
- **Virtual Reality:** VRChat is designed primarily for VR headsets, offering an immersive social experience. It also supports non-VR users.

- **Avatar Customization:** Users can create highly customized avatars using 3D modeling software, allowing for a diverse range of expressions and identities.

**User Experience:**
- **Social Interaction:** VRChat focuses on social interaction, with users exploring virtual worlds, attending events, and participating in group activities.

- **User-Created Worlds:** The platform supports user-generated content, with tools for creating and sharing custom worlds and experiences.

**Economic Model:**

- **Free to Play:** VRChat is free to download and use, with a premium subscription model offering additional features and customization options.

- **In-App Purchases:** Users can purchase items and accessories for their avatars and virtual environments.

**Challenges:**

- **Content Moderation:** Managing user behavior and content to maintain a safe and respectful community is a continuous challenge.

- **Technical Stability:** Ensuring a smooth and stable experience for users, particularly in VR, requires ongoing technical improvements.

## 5. Somnium Space

Somnium Space is a decentralized VR platform that aims to create a fully immersive and persistent virtual world, with a strong emphasis on user ownership and blockchain integration.

**Technological Foundation:**
- **Full Immersion:** Somnium Space offers a highly immersive VR experience, with a focus on realism and user interaction.

- **Blockchain Integration:** The platform uses blockchain technology to enable ownership of virtual land and assets through NFTs.

**User Experience:**
- **Persistent World:** Somnium Space features a persistent virtual world, meaning that changes made by users remain even when they log off.

- **Customization and Creation:** Users can build and customize their virtual environments, creating unique experiences and interactions.

**Economic Model:**

- **Cryptocurrency:** The platform uses its native cryptocurrency, Somnium Cubes (CUBES), for transactions. Users can buy, sell, and trade virtual land and assets.

- **Virtual Real Estate:** Owning and developing virtual land is a key component of the Somnium Space economy, with land parcels traded as NFTs.

**Challenges:**

- **User Base:** Growing and sustaining a large and active user base is essential for the platform's success.

- **Technical and Financial Barriers:** High-quality VR experiences require substantial technical infrastructure and investment, which can be a barrier for some users and developers.

The Metaverse is rapidly evolving, with platforms like Second Life, Decentraland, Roblox, VRChat, and Somnium Space leading the way. Each platform offers unique features and experiences, driven by different technological foundations, user experiences, and economic models. While the opportunities for innovation and engagement are vast, challenges such as scalability, content moderation, user adoption, and technical stability must be addressed to ensure the sustainable growth of these virtual worlds. By understanding the strengths and limitations of these existing platforms, stakeholders can better navigate the development and integration of the Metaverse, creating immersive, inclusive, and secure digital environments for users worldwide.

## ➢ Metaverse Development Success Stories and Failures to Learn from

There are many inspiring success stories and sobering failure stories in the developing Metaverse. Developers, companies, and stakeholders can learn a lot about what makes projects successful and how to steer clear of typical mistakes by looking at these situations. This section will examine prominent achievements and noteworthy setbacks in the creation of the Metaverse, emphasising important lessons learned from each.

- **Achievements**

**1. Roblox: Strengthening Content Created by Users**

Roblox is a user-generated content platform that was introduced in 2006 and lets users make and play games made by other users. With millions of active users, it has expanded into a multibillion dollar business.

**Key Success Factors:**
- **User-Generated Content:** Roblox's main advantage is its capacity to tap into its users' inventiveness. Roblox makes game development accessible and offers strong tools, which have allowed for a wide variety of experiences and long-term involvement.

- **Cross-Platform Accessibility:** Roblox is widely accessible and has a growing user base due to its availability on a variety of platforms, including PCs, mobile devices, and gaming consoles.

**- Monetization Model:** Developers can profitably market their works by using Robux, the platform's virtual currency. This gives Roblox and its developers an income stream and encourages the production of high-quality content.

**- Community and Social Features:** With features like chat, buddy lists, and cooperative development, the platform fosters a strong sense of community by emphasising social interaction.

**Takeaways:**

**- Empowering Users:** Giving people the means and autonomy to produce can result in a thriving and self-sufficient ecosystem.

**- Accessibility:** A platform's appeal and user base can be greatly expanded by making sure it is available on a variety of devices.

**- Incentivization:** A cleverly thought-out monetization plan can encourage users to produce excellent content and sustain interaction.

## 2. Decentraland: Establishing Virtual Ownership with Blockchain Technology

Users can buy, develop, and trade virtual land as NFTs in Decentraland, a decentralised virtual world constructed on the Ethereum blockchain. Its creative use of blockchain technology has drawn a lot of attention.

**Key Success Factors:**
**- Blockchain Integration:** Decentraland secures real ownership of digital assets through the use of blockchain technology, giving users verifiable and transferable virtual property.

**- Decentralised Governance:** A decentralised autonomous organisation (DAO) oversees the platform's governance, giving users a voice in its development and policies.

**- Virtual Real Estate Market:** Developers and investors are drawn to the burgeoning virtual real estate market because it is possible to purchase, sell, and develop virtual land.

**- Events and Community Activities:** Organising online gatherings and encouraging community initiatives have aided in sustaining user participation and drawing in new members.

**Takeaways:**

**- Intelligent Technology:** Using state-of-the-art technology such as blockchain can produce distinctive value propositions and draw in a loyal user base.

**- User Governance:** Encouraging user participation in governance can strengthen ties to the community and guarantee that the platform changes to suit user requirements.

- **Virtual Economy:** Creating a dynamic virtual economy with real-world value can drive engagement and investment.

### 3. VRChat: Fostering Social Interaction in VR

VRChat is a social VR platform that enables users to interact in a variety of virtual worlds using custom avatars. It has become a popular destination for social interaction in virtual reality.

**Key Success Factors:**
- **Immersive Social Experience:** VRChat provides a highly immersive social experience, allowing users to communicate and interact in ways that mimic real-life interactions.

- **User-Created Worlds:** The platform supports user-generated content, with users building and sharing custom worlds and experiences.

- **Avatar Customization:** Extensive avatar customization options enable users to express their identities and creativity fully.

- **Community Events:** Regular community events and activities help maintain user engagement and build a strong sense of community.

**Lessons Learned:**
- **Immersive Interaction:** Providing immersive and interactive experiences can significantly enhance user engagement.

- **User Creativity:** Encouraging user-generated content can lead to a diverse and continuously evolving platform.

- **Community Building:** Fostering a strong community through events and social features can drive long-term engagement.

- **Learning from Failures**

**1. Google Lively: Overcoming Initial Hurdles**

Google Lively was a web-based virtual world launched in 2008 that allowed users to create and decorate virtual rooms and interact with others. It was shut down after just a few months.

**Key Failures:**
- **Lack of Clear Value Proposition:** Google Lively struggled to differentiate itself from other social platforms and failed to provide a compelling reason for users to switch from existing services.

- **Technical Limitations:** The platform faced significant technical issues, including performance problems and limited interactivity, which hindered user experience.

- **Insufficient Community Engagement:** Lively lacked features that encouraged community building and sustained user engagement, leading to rapid user attrition.

**Lessons Learned:**

- **Unique Value Proposition:** Platforms need a clear and compelling value proposition to attract and retain users.

- **Technical Robustness:** Ensuring technical stability and performance is crucial for maintaining user satisfaction.

- **Community Focus:** Building features that foster community interaction and engagement is essential for long-term success.

**2. Sansar: Navigating Market Expectations**

Sansar, developed by Linden Lab (the creators of Second Life), aimed to create a new social VR platform. Despite initial excitement, it struggled to gain traction and was eventually sold to a new company.

**Key Failures:**

- **Over-Reliance on VR:** Sansar heavily focused on VR, which limited its accessibility to users without VR headsets, reducing its potential user base.

- **High Expectations:** The platform faced high expectations due to Linden Lab's reputation, which it struggled to meet, leading to disappointment among early adopters.

- **Economic Model:** Sansar's monetization strategies were not well-received by users, and it failed to establish a robust virtual economy.

**Lessons Learned:**

- **Broad Accessibility:** Ensuring that a platform is accessible to a wide range of users, including those without specialized hardware, can broaden its appeal.

- **Managing Expectations:** Setting realistic expectations and delivering on promises is crucial for maintaining user trust.

- **Effective Monetization:** Developing a user-friendly and effective monetization model is key to sustaining a virtual economy.

The journey of Metaverse development is marked by both inspiring successes and instructive failures. By examining these cases, developers and stakeholders can understand the critical factors that contribute to success, such as empowering user creativity, leveraging innovative technologies, and fostering strong communities. At the same time, they can learn to avoid common pitfalls like technical limitations, lack of a clear value proposition, and inadequate user engagement strategies. Ultimately, the insights gained from these success stories and failures will guide the future development of the Metaverse, helping to create immersive, inclusive, and thriving virtual worlds.

➤ **Interviews with Metaverse Development Industry Leaders**

Leaders in the field can be interviewed to gain important insights about the present and future of Metaverse development. These discussions shed light on the goals, difficulties, and inventions propelling the Metaverse as well as the tactics used by effective leaders. An overview of major industry players' thoughts on several facets of Metaverse development may be seen below.

**1. Philip Rosedale, Second Life's founder**

One of the first virtual worlds, Second Life, was founded by Philip Rosedale. His contributions have had a big impact on how online virtual environments are being developed.

**Key Takeaways:**

- **Vision for the Metaverse:** According to Rosedale, the Metaverse is an extension of the internet, with immersive 3D places serving as new frontiers for business, creativity, and social interaction. According to him, decentralised ownership and user-generated content would be the driving forces behind the Metaverse.

- **Challenges and Solutions:** Rosedale states that ensuring a consistent user experience across several virtual worlds is a major obstacle in the creation of the Metaverse. He highlights the necessity of standards and interoperability to guarantee seamless user movement and interaction across multiple platforms.

- **Future Trends:** Rosedale emphasises how increasingly immersive experiences may be created with the help of virtual reality (VR) and augmented reality (AR) technologies. He also emphasises how important blockchain technology is to maintaining digital property rights and conducting business inside the Metaverse.

## 2. Journey's Chief Metaverse Officer, Cathy Hackl

Cathy Hackl is a well-known personality in the Metaverse industry, well recognised for her contributions to VR/AR and her position as Chief Metaverse Officer of Journey, a business that creates Metaverse experiences.

**Key Takeaways:**

- **User Experience:** Hackl stresses the significance of designing user interfaces that are simple to use and easily accessible. She emphasises that the Metaverse should be made as user-friendly as possible, with a focus on lowering entrance barriers for potential new users.

- **AI Integration:** Hackl talks about how AI may improve the Metaverse by offering more individualised and engaging experiences. A few examples of how AI is being included are adaptive surroundings, intelligent virtual assistants, and avatars driven by AI.

- **Diversity and Inclusion:** Noting that a varied range of views and perspectives will make the virtual world richer and more representative, Hackl promotes diversity and inclusion in the Metaverse. She urges the implementation of inclusive design principles to guarantee accessibility for every user.

**3. Epic Games' CEO, Tim Sweeney**

A major figure in the gaming industry and an advocate of the Metaverse is Tim Sweeney, the CEO of Epic Games. The Unreal Engine developed by his firm is an essential tool for creating virtual worlds of superior quality.

**Key Takeaways:**

- **Technological Innovation:** Sweeney emphasises how real-time rendering and sophisticated graphics contribute to the creation of realistic and engrossing virtual environments. He underlines that ongoing improvements in processing power and graphics technology will be advantageous to the Metaverse.

- **Economic Opportunities:** According to Sweeney, businesses and developers will have access to new markets as a result of the Metaverse. In his ideal future, new monetization strategies will emerge and virtual goods and services will play a crucial role in the development of the digital economy.

- **Collaboration and Standards:** Sweeney encourages industry participants to work together to develop uniform guidelines and conventions. He thinks that building a coherent and interoperable Metaverse will require a unified strategy.

## 4. Yat Siu, Animoca Brands' co-founder and chairman

Yat Siu is the chairman and co-founder of Animoca Brands, a blockchain-based gaming and virtual worlds company. He is a strong proponent of the Metaverse's incorporation of blockchain technology.

**Key Insights:**

**- Blockchain and NFTs:** Siu highlights how blockchain technology and non-fungible tokens (NFTs) in the Metaverse have the ability to revolutionise. According to him, NFTs will make it possible for people to truly own digital assets and develop new business models for virtual goods and services.

**- User Empowerment:** Siu supports decentralisation and user empowerment in the Metaverse. Rather than relying on centralised platforms, he sees a future where users have more control over their virtual assets and experiences.

**- Regulatory Considerations:** Siu recognises that in order to handle concerns about digital ownership and transactions, regulatory frameworks are necessary. He calls for balanced regulations that protect users while fostering innovation.

## 5. Mark Zuckerberg - CEO of Meta (formerly Facebook)

Mark Zuckerberg, CEO of Meta, is a major proponent of the Metaverse and has invested heavily in its development through his company's initiatives.

**Key Insights:**

- **Metaverse Vision:** Zuckerberg's vision for the Metaverse is centered around creating a fully immersive digital space where people can connect, work, and play. He sees the Metaverse as a natural extension of social media, enhancing the ways people interact and collaborate online.

- **Technological Development:** Zuckerberg discusses the importance of developing advanced VR and AR technologies to enable more immersive and realistic experiences. He highlights ongoing efforts to improve hardware, software, and network infrastructure to support the Metaverse.

- **Privacy and Safety:** Zuckerberg acknowledges the importance of addressing privacy and safety concerns in the Metaverse. He emphasizes the need for robust data protection measures and user controls to ensure a secure and respectful environment.

Interviews with industry leaders provide a comprehensive view of the Metaverse's current landscape and future potential. These experts share valuable insights into the technological, economic, and social aspects of Metaverse development.

Their opinions underscore the importance of innovation, user experience, and collaboration in creating the future of virtual worlds. As the Metaverse continues to evolve, the lessons and visions shared by these leaders will play a crucial role in guiding its development and ensuring its success.

# Chapter Eight

# Upcoming Developments and Trends in the Metaverse

Both changes in user behaviour and technology improvements are causing the Metaverse to evolve quickly. A number of upcoming trends and advancements will probably influence the direction of this digital frontier as it grows. The Metaverse's future is full with promising prospects as well as formidable obstacles, from societal conventions to technology advancements. This is a detailed look at what to anticipate.

## 1. Technological Developments

### Augmented Reality (AR) and Enhanced Virtual Reality (VR)

The advancement of VR and AR technology will remain a key factor in the expansion of the Metaverse. Future virtual reality headsets should have better tracking, resolution, and field of view in addition to being lighter, more comfortable, and more immersive. With the increasing integration of AR technology into daily life, users will be able to easily superimpose digital content on the real world. By fusing virtual and real-world elements, this convergence of VR and AR will produce more interactive and immersive experiences in the Metaverse.

**Better Infrastructure and Connectivity**

The Metaverse experience will be greatly enhanced by 5G and beyond, which will offer quicker and more dependable internet connectivity. Real-time interactivity and high-quality VR and AR content streaming will be supported by this. Furthermore, cloud computing advances will make it easier to create expansive, dynamic virtual worlds that require a lot of processing power. Additionally, edge computing will proliferate as a means of cutting latency and enhancing user experience globally.

## Machine learning and artificial intelligence (AI)

The Metaverse will be profoundly impacted by AI and machine learning since they will make virtual environments more complex and flexible. More realistic and customised interactions will be provided by AI-driven characters and NPCs (non-player characters). Algorithms for machine learning will improve content creation tools, making it easier for users to create intricate virtual worlds and assets. AI will also be involved in content moderation and making sure that users are in a polite and safe environment.

## Decentralisation and Blockchain

Blockchain technology, which offers a basis for safe and open transactions, will remain a fundamental component of the Metaverse. True ownership of digital assets will be made possible by non-fungible tokens (NFTs), while smart contracts will enable sophisticated interactions and agreements within the Metaverse. A more transparent and inclusive digital economy will be promoted by the use of decentralised finance (DeFi) and decentralised autonomous organisations (DAOs), which will enable users to engage in economic and governmental processes.

## 2. Changing User Attitudes

**Individualization and Tailoring**

Thanks to developments in AI and data analytics, the Metaverse will provide experiences that are progressively more tailored. Users will be able to tailor their virtual environments, avatars, and interactions to reflect their individual preferences and identities. Enhanced customization options will allow users to create unique and meaningful virtual experiences, contributing to a more engaging and immersive Metaverse.

**Social Interaction and Collaboration**

The way people interact and collaborate in the Metaverse will evolve, with new forms of social engagement emerging. Virtual meetings, events, and gatherings will become more common, supported by advanced VR and AR technologies. Collaborative workplaces will enable distant teams to work together more effectively, breaking down geographical borders and boosting global cooperation. Social features such as virtual hangouts, shared experiences, and community-driven activities will strengthen connections and create vibrant virtual communities.

**Entertainment and Media**

The entertainment industry will continue to play a significant role in the Metaverse, with virtual concerts, live events, and immersive experiences becoming mainstream. Content creators will explore new formats and storytelling techniques, leveraging the interactive capabilities of the Metaverse to engage audiences in innovative ways. Virtual reality gaming, interactive movies, and augmented reality experiences will blur the lines between traditional media and digital entertainment.

**Education and Training**

Education and training will benefit from the immersive and interactive capabilities of the Metaverse. Virtual classrooms and training environments will provide hands-on learning experiences that simulate real-world scenarios. Institutions will adopt VR and AR technologies to create engaging educational content and enable remote learning. The Metaverse will also support professional development by offering realistic simulations and collaborative training tools for various industries.

### 3. Economic Opportunities and Challenges

**Virtual Economies and Digital Assets**

The Metaverse will continue to drive the growth of virtual economies, with new business models and revenue streams emerging. Digital assets such as virtual real estate, NFTs, and in-game currencies will play a central role in the economy of the Metaverse. Businesses and entrepreneurs will explore innovative ways to monetize virtual experiences and assets, creating opportunities for investment and entrepreneurship.

## Regulatory and Legal Issues

As the Metaverse expands, regulatory and legal challenges will become more prominent. Issues related to intellectual property, data privacy, and digital rights will need to be addressed. Governments and regulatory bodies will work to develop frameworks that balance innovation with protection for users. The Metaverse community will also need to establish ethical guidelines and best practices to ensure a fair and inclusive digital environment.

## Inclusivity and Accessibility

Ensuring that the Metaverse is inclusive and accessible to all users will be a critical consideration. Developers will need to address issues related to digital divide, accessibility, and representation. Efforts to create diverse and equitable virtual spaces will help ensure that the Metaverse serves as a platform for everyone, regardless of background or ability.

## Sustainability and Environmental Impact

The environmental impact of Metaverse technologies will be a growing concern. The energy consumption associated with VR/AR hardware, data centers, and blockchain networks will need to be addressed. Efforts to develop more energy-efficient technologies and sustainable practices will be essential in mitigating the environmental footprint of the Metaverse.

## 4. Cultural and Societal Implications

### Redefining Social Norms

The Metaverse will challenge and redefine traditional social norms and behaviors. Virtual interactions will influence how people perceive and experience relationships, identity, and community. The development of social etiquette and norms for virtual environments will be an ongoing process, shaping how users engage with each other and navigate digital spaces.

**Impact on Work and Employment**

The Metaverse will transform the nature of work and employment, with new job roles and opportunities emerging in virtual environments. Remote work will become more prevalent, supported by virtual workspaces and collaboration tools. The rise of virtual entrepreneurship and digital asset management will create new career paths and economic opportunities.

**Mental Health and Well-being**

The impact of the Metaverse on mental health and well-being will be a key consideration. While virtual environments can offer positive experiences and support social connections, there is also the potential for negative effects, such as social isolation or addiction. Addressing these challenges will require ongoing research and the development of strategies to promote healthy and balanced engagement with the Metaverse.

The future of the Metaverse is filled with potential and promise, driven by technological advancements, evolving user experiences, and new economic opportunities. As the Metaverse continues to develop, it will present both exciting possibilities and significant challenges. By staying informed about emerging trends and addressing critical issues, stakeholders can help shape a Metaverse that is innovative, inclusive, and impactful. The journey ahead will be shaped by collaboration, creativity, and a shared vision for the future of digital spaces.

## ➢ New Developments and Technologies in the Metaverse

The Metaverse is changing quickly, and new ideas and technologies will have a major impact on how it develops in the future. A number of significant technological developments and breakthroughs will revolutionise user interaction with virtual environments, content creation and consumption, and business practices as the Metaverse grows. This is a summary of the most significant new technologies and inventions that are advancing the Metaverse.

## 1. Enhanced Augmented Reality (AR) and Virtual Reality (VR)

**Improved VR Equipment**

Virtual reality experiences are becoming more accessible and engaging thanks to advancements in VR gear. With better tracking capabilities, a larger field of view, and higher resolution screens, new VR headsets are currently under development. Innovations that improve user comfort and mobility include wireless connectivity and lightweight designs. Furthermore, more responsive and intuitive interactions are being made possible by haptic feedback and eye-tracking technologies, which give users a stronger sense of presence in virtual environments.

**Integration of AR**

The integration of augmented reality (AR) technology into commonplace gadgets like tablets, smartphones, and AR glasses is growing. These developments are making it easier for people to superimpose digital data on the real environment. Applications in retail, entertainment, education, and navigation are being supported by enhanced augmented reality experiences. The smooth transition between virtual and physical elements is increasing user engagement and broadening the range of possible applications for augmented reality in the Metaverse.

## 2. Machine learning and artificial intelligence (AI)

### AI-Powered NPCs and Avatars

Artificial Intelligence is transforming the creation and interaction of virtual environments and characters. Artificial intelligence (AI)-powered avatars and non-player characters (NPCs) can react intelligently to user interactions and display realistic behaviours. Thanks to these developments, users can now enjoy more dynamic and customised interactions in the Metaverse, where virtual characters can offer assistance, company, and interactive storytelling.

**Content Generation and Personalization**

Machine learning algorithms are enhancing content creation tools, allowing users to generate complex virtual environments and assets more efficiently. AI-driven systems can analyze user preferences and behaviors to deliver personalized content and recommendations. This capability is fostering more engaging and tailored experiences in the Metaverse, as users encounter content that aligns with their interests and needs.

**3. Blockchain and Decentralization**

**A. Non-Fungible Tokens (NFTs)**

Blockchain technology, particularly through the use of non-fungible tokens (NFTs), is transforming the concept of ownership and value in the Metaverse. NFTs enable users to own and trade unique digital assets, such as virtual real estate, artwork, and collectibles. This innovation is creating new economic opportunities and business models, allowing users to invest in and monetize virtual assets.

**Decentralized Finance (DeFi)**

Decentralized finance (DeFi) is introducing new financial systems and services within the Metaverse. DeFi platforms leverage blockchain technology to offer financial products such as lending, borrowing, and trading without the need for traditional intermediaries. This innovation is fostering a more open and accessible financial ecosystem, where users can participate in economic activities and manage digital assets securely.

**Decentralized Autonomous Organizations (DAOs)**

Decentralized autonomous organizations (DAOs) are facilitating community governance and decision-making in the Metaverse. DAOs use blockchain-based smart contracts to enable transparent and democratic management of virtual assets and projects. This innovation empowers users to have a voice in the development and governance of virtual environments, promoting a more inclusive and collaborative Metaverse.

## 4. 5G and Edge Computing

**Enhanced Connectivity**

5G technology is providing the high-speed, low-latency connectivity needed for immersive Metaverse experiences. The increased bandwidth and reduced latency of 5G networks are supporting real-time interactions, high-quality streaming, and complex virtual environments. As 5G becomes more widespread, it will enable smoother and more responsive experiences in the Metaverse, regardless of location.

**Edge Computing**

Edge computing is complementing 5G by bringing computational resources closer to users. By processing data at the edge of the network, rather than relying solely on centralized data centers, edge computing reduces latency and improves performance. This technology is essential for handling the large volumes of data generated by VR/AR applications and ensuring seamless and efficient interactions in the Metaverse.

## 5. Spatial Computing

**Immersive Interaction**

Spatial computing is redefining how users interact with virtual and physical spaces. By integrating 3D spatial data and context-aware computing, spatial computing enables more intuitive and immersive experiences in the Metaverse. Users can interact with digital objects and environments in a way that mirrors real-world interactions, enhancing the sense of presence and engagement.

**Gesture and Voice Recognition**

Advancements in gesture and voice recognition technologies are allowing users to interact with virtual environments more naturally. These technologies enable hands-free control and communication, reducing reliance on traditional input devices such as keyboards and controllers. As gesture and voice recognition become more sophisticated, they will enhance the usability and accessibility of the Metaverse.

## 6. Quantum Computing

**Enhanced Computational Power**

Quantum computing is poised to revolutionize the Metaverse by providing unprecedented computational power. Quantum computers have the potential to solve complex problems and perform calculations at speeds far beyond current classical computers. This capability could enable more advanced simulations, improve AI algorithms, and enhance the overall performance and scalability of the Metaverse.

**Cryptographic Advances**

Quantum computing also has implications for cryptography and data security. As quantum computers become more powerful, they may challenge existing encryption methods. This necessitates the development of quantum-resistant cryptographic techniques to protect data and transactions in the Metaverse. Researchers and developers are working to ensure that future quantum computing advances do not compromise the security and privacy of virtual environments.

## 7. Sustainability and Green Technologies

### Energy-Efficient Technologies

As the Metaverse grows, addressing its environmental impact will become increasingly important. Innovations in energy-efficient technologies and sustainable practices will be essential for reducing the carbon footprint of virtual environments. Developments in green data centers, energy-efficient hardware, and eco-friendly blockchain technologies are contributing to a more sustainable Metaverse.

### Circular Economy

The concept of a circular economy is gaining traction in the Metaverse, where the focus is on reducing waste and maximizing resource efficiency. Projects including repurposing virtual materials, recycling digital assets, and reducing electronic waste are being investigated. Embracing circular economy principles will help ensure that the Metaverse evolves in an environmentally responsible manner.

The future of the Metaverse is being shaped by a range of emerging technologies and innovations. From advancements in VR/AR and AI to the integration of blockchain and quantum computing, these developments are driving the evolution of virtual environments and experiences. As the Metaverse continues to grow, staying informed about these trends and innovations will be crucial for harnessing their potential and addressing associated challenges. The ongoing exploration and integration of these technologies will play a pivotal role in shaping the future of the Metaverse and its impact on society.

## ➢ Future Forecasts for the Metaverse

With its innovative blend of virtual and physical realities, the Metaverse promises to transform a number of facets of daily life, work, and entertainment. It marks a new frontier in digital interaction. It is anticipated that the Metaverse will change significantly as society norms and technology advance. The following are some major forecasts for the Metaverse's future:

## 1. Integration and Mainstream Adoption

**Widespread Use and Access**

It is anticipated that the Metaverse will gain widespread traction in the upcoming years, catering to a wide range of industries and demographics. People will use VR/AR technologies for work, entertainment, and social interaction more frequently as they become more widely available and reasonably priced. Virtual worlds will permeate daily life more and more, enhancing rather than taking the place of in-person interactions.

**Integrated with the Physical World Seamlessly**

The line separating the real world from the virtual world will only get fuzzier. Technologies such as augmented reality (AR) will overlay digital information onto physical spaces, while virtual reality (VR) will offer immersive experiences that complement real-world activities. This integration will enhance daily experiences, from virtual shopping and entertainment to remote work and education.

## 2. Economic Expansion and New Business Models

### Growth of Virtual Economies

Virtual economies will increase dramatically, with digital assets, cryptocurrencies, and virtual items becoming crucial to economic interactions. Virtual real estate, non-fungible tokens (NFTs), and digital collectibles will expand in value and relevance, offering new investment and revenue options. Businesses will develop novel revenue models tailored to the Metaverse, leveraging virtual storefronts, experiences, and services.

### Emergence of New Industries and Jobs

There will be new sectors and occupations created by the Metaverse. There will be a growing number of people pursuing careers in virtual event management, digital asset creation, and virtual architecture. Furthermore, positions pertaining to the administration and control of virtual environments, along with the creation of applications tailored to the Metaverse, will surface. Within the Metaverse, this expansion will promote economic growth and innovation.

## 3. Technological Advancements

**Enhanced Immersion and Interactivity**

Future advancements in VR and AR technologies will lead to even greater immersion and interactivity. Improved hardware, such as more advanced VR headsets and AR glasses, will offer higher resolution, wider fields of view, and more realistic sensory feedback. Innovations in haptic technology and eye-tracking will further enhance the realism and engagement of virtual experiences.

**Integration of AI and Machine Learning**

Artificial intelligence (AI) and machine learning will play a critical role in the Metaverse, enabling more dynamic and responsive virtual environments. AI-driven avatars and non-player characters (NPCs) will exhibit more realistic behavior and interactions, while machine learning algorithms will personalize content and experiences based on user preferences. These advancements will contribute to a more engaging and adaptive Metaverse.

## Blockchain and Decentralization

Blockchain technology will continue to be a cornerstone of the Metaverse, supporting secure transactions and decentralized governance. Smart contracts and decentralized autonomous organizations (DAOs) will facilitate transparent and efficient interactions, while NFTs will provide verifiable ownership of digital assets. The emphasis on decentralization will empower users and creators, promoting a more open and participatory digital economy.

## 4. Social and Cultural Impact

## Transformation of Social Interactions

The Metaverse will transform social interactions, offering new ways to connect, collaborate, and communicate. Virtual spaces will become social hubs where people can meet, socialize, and participate in shared experiences. The development of new social norms and etiquettes will shape how individuals engage with each other in the Metaverse, influencing relationships and community dynamics.

**Redefinition of Identity and Presence**

The Metaverse will offer new opportunities for self-expression and identity exploration. Users will have the ability to create and customize digital avatars that represent different aspects of their personalities. The concept of presence will evolve as people navigate virtual environments, experiencing new forms of interaction and immersion that challenge traditional notions of identity and social presence.

**Impact on Education and Training**

Education and training will be transformed by the Metaverse, providing immersive and interactive learning experiences. Virtual classrooms, simulations, and training environments will offer hands-on learning opportunities that mirror real-world scenarios. Educational institutions and organizations will leverage the Metaverse to enhance learning outcomes, facilitate remote education, and foster collaborative skills development.

## 5. Privacy and Security Concerns

### Data Privacy and Protection

As the Metaverse grows, concerns about data privacy and protection will intensify. The collection and management of personal data within virtual environments will require robust security measures and transparent practices. Ensuring user privacy and safeguarding sensitive information will be critical to maintaining trust and integrity in the Metaverse.

### Security Threats and Challenges

The Metaverse will face various security threats, including cyberattacks, identity theft, and fraud. Protecting virtual assets and ensuring secure transactions will be essential for mitigating risks and maintaining a safe digital environment. The development of advanced security protocols and technologies will be necessary to address emerging threats and challenges.

## 6. Regulatory and Ethical Considerations

### Development of Regulatory Frameworks

Governments and regulatory bodies will work to establish frameworks for governing the Metaverse, addressing issues related to intellectual property, digital rights, and online behavior. Balancing innovation with regulation will be essential for fostering a healthy and equitable Metaverse while protecting users and stakeholders.

### Ethical Implications

The ethical implications of Metaverse interactions will be a focal point of discussion. Issues such as digital equity, representation, and inclusivity will require attention to ensure that the Metaverse serves as a fair and accessible platform for all users. Addressing ethical concerns will involve creating guidelines and best practices for responsible behavior and interaction within virtual environments.

The future of the Metaverse promises to be dynamic and

transformative, driven by technological advancements, evolving social interactions, and expanding economic opportunities. As the Metaverse continues to develop, stakeholders will need to navigate a complex landscape of innovation, privacy, and regulation. By staying informed about emerging trends and addressing key challenges, we can shape a Metaverse that is inclusive, secure, and impactful. The journey ahead will require collaboration, creativity, and a shared vision for the future of digital spaces.

## ➢ Preparing for What's Next in the Metaverse

As the Metaverse continues to evolve and integrate into various aspects of life, businesses, individuals, and organizations must prepare for its future impact. This preparation involves understanding emerging trends, adapting to new technologies, and addressing potential challenges. Here's a guide to navigating the next phases of Metaverse development and ensuring readiness for what's ahead.

## 1. Stay Informed and Educated

### Continuous Learning

The Metaverse is a rapidly evolving space, and staying informed about the latest developments is crucial. Engage in continuous learning through industry publications, webinars, conferences, and online courses. Understanding emerging technologies, trends, and best practices will help you stay ahead of the curve and adapt to changes effectively.

### Networking and Collaboration

Build a network of professionals and experts in the Metaverse field. Join industry forums, attend events, and participate in discussions to exchange ideas and insights. Collaboration with peers and thought leaders can provide valuable perspectives and foster opportunities for innovation and growth.

## 2. Embrace Technological Advancements

### Invest in Emerging Technologies

Be proactive in adopting and experimenting with emerging technologies that are shaping the Metaverse. This includes investing in advanced VR/AR hardware, exploring blockchain applications, and leveraging AI and machine learning. By integrating these technologies into your projects and strategies, you can enhance capabilities and create cutting-edge experiences.

### Develop and Test Prototypes

Before fully committing to new technologies, develop and test prototypes to assess their feasibility and impact. Prototyping allows you to experiment with new ideas, refine concepts, and identify potential challenges. This iterative approach will help you make informed decisions and optimize your Metaverse initiatives.

## 3. Focus on User Experience and Engagement

**Prioritize User-Centered Design**

Design experiences and applications with a focus on user needs and preferences. Conduct user research, gather feedback, and iterate on designs to ensure that your offerings are engaging, intuitive, and accessible. A user-centered approach will enhance satisfaction and drive adoption in the Metaverse.

**Create Immersive and Interactive Content**

Develop content that leverages the full potential of the Metaverse's immersive and interactive capabilities. This includes creating engaging virtual environments, interactive simulations, and dynamic storytelling experiences. High-quality content will attract and retain users, fostering a vibrant and active Metaverse community.

## 4. Address Privacy and Security Concerns

**Implement Robust Security Measures**

Ensure that your Metaverse applications and platforms adhere to the highest security standards. Implement strong encryption, secure authentication, and regular vulnerability assessments to protect user data and prevent cyberattacks. Prioritizing security will build trust and safeguard your users' information.

**Promote Privacy Best Practices**

Adopt privacy best practices and comply with relevant regulations to protect user privacy. Be transparent about data collection, usage, and storage practices. Provide users with control over their personal information and offer clear options for managing privacy settings.

## 5. Adapt to Regulatory and Ethical Challenges

**Stay Compliant with Regulations**

Monitor and comply with regulatory developments related to the Metaverse. This includes data protection laws, intellectual property regulations, and digital rights. Staying informed about regulatory changes and adapting your practices accordingly will help you navigate legal challenges and avoid potential pitfalls.

**Address Ethical Considerations**

Be mindful of the ethical implications of Metaverse interactions. Promote inclusivity, diversity, and fairness in your virtual environments. Address issues related to digital equity, representation, and user behavior to create a positive and respectful Metaverse experience.

## 6. Prepare for Economic and Business Impacts

**Explore New Business Models**

Innovate and explore new business models tailored to the Metaverse. This includes virtual storefronts, subscription services, and digital asset marketplaces. By adapting to new economic opportunities, you can capitalize on the growth of virtual economies and drive revenue in the Metaverse.

### Assess Financial Implications

Evaluate the financial implications of your Metaverse initiatives, including investment costs, potential revenue streams, and return on investment. Develop a financial strategy that aligns with your goals and ensures sustainable growth in the Metaverse.

## 7. Foster a Culture of Innovation

### Encourage Creativity and Experimentation

Promote a culture of innovation and experimentation within your organization. Encourage teams to explore new ideas, take risks, and embrace emerging trends. Fostering creativity will drive innovation and help you stay ahead in the competitive Metaverse landscape.

### Support Ongoing Research and Development

Invest in research and development to stay at the forefront of Metaverse advancements. Support projects that explore new technologies, applications, and user experiences. Ongoing R&D will enable you to adapt to changing trends and contribute to the evolution of the

Metaverse.

## 8. Plan for Long-Term Sustainability

**Consider Environmental Impact**

Address the environmental impact of your Metaverse activities. Explore sustainable practices, such as energy-efficient technologies and eco-friendly data centers. Contributing to a greener Metaverse will align with broader sustainability goals and appeal to environmentally conscious users.

**Develop Scalable Solutions**

Design solutions that are scalable and adaptable to future developments. Consider the long-term growth and evolution of the Metaverse when planning and implementing your projects. Scalable solutions will ensure that your initiatives remain relevant and effective as the Metaverse expands.

Preparing for the future of the Metaverse involves staying informed, embracing technological advancements, focusing on user experience, addressing privacy and security concerns, adapting to regulatory and ethical challenges, exploring economic opportunities, fostering innovation, and planning for long-term sustainability. By proactively addressing these areas, you can navigate the evolving Metaverse landscape and position yourself for success in this dynamic and transformative space. As the Metaverse continues to develop, your readiness and adaptability will be key to thriving in this exciting new frontier.

# Conclusion

The Metaverse is a revolutionary development in digital interaction that combines virtual and real-world elements to create dynamic, immersive worlds that have the potential to drastically alter many facets of work, play, and daily life. It is evident that the Metaverse has the power to drastically change how we interact, produce, and do business in the digital age as we stand on the cusp of this new frontier. However, manoeuvring across this intricate and dynamic landscape calls for considerable thought, planning, and adaptation.

- **Adopting the Possibilities**

The Metaverse offers a plethora of diverse and expansive opportunities. The Metaverse provides an unprecedented platform for invention and growth, enabling the creation of new forms of entertainment and education as well as revolutionising social relationships and economic models. Through the adoption of cutting-edge technologies like blockchain, augmented reality, virtual reality, and the Internet of Things (IoT), people and organisations can discover new avenues for growth and produce memorable experiences.

Technological breakthroughs will keep propelling the Metaverse's development, making ever-more immersive and interactive settings possible. As VR and AR technology progress and become more widely available, virtual experiences will become more realistic and of higher quality. The Metaverse will become more responsive and engaging as a result of AI and machine learning personalising interactions and information. IoT will smoothly merge the real and virtual worlds, while blockchain technology will enable safe transactions and digital asset ownership.

These technologies will create new prospects for economic opportunities and business innovation as they develop. The growth of virtual economies will open up new markets for digital products and services. The Metaverse will provide chances for virtual stores, subscription services, and digital asset trading, requiring business models to adjust accordingly. The emergence of

NFTs and virtual real estate will change the economic landscape by bringing in new sources of income and investment.

- **Handling the Difficulties**

The Metaverse has amazing potential, but there are a number of issues that need to be resolved. Since the gathering and handling of personal data in virtual environments raises questions about data protection and cyber threats, ensuring **privacy and security** is crucial. Retaining user confidence and protecting data will require putting strong security measures in place and encouraging best practices in privacy.

Ethical and regulatory factors will be pivotal in determining how the Metaverse develops. Regulatory frameworks pertaining to digital rights, intellectual property, and online behaviour will require adjustments as the Metaverse expands. In order to create a welcoming and fair virtual environment, ethical factors such as inclusivity, representation, and responsible behaviour are essential.

There will also be substantial **social and cultural impacts**. People's interactions, connections, and self-expression will change as a result of the Metaverse, creating new social norms and cultural dynamics. It will be essential to comprehend these shifts and promote an innovative and creative culture if we are to adjust to and influence the Metaverse's future development.

- **Getting Ready for What's to Come**

In order to adequately get ready for the Metaverse's future, people and institutions should concentrate on the following important areas:

**1. Remain Informed and Educated:** It's critical to keep up-to-date on the latest developments in technology and trends. To stay current and informed, read industry publications, go to events, and take part in conversations.

**2. Welcome Technological Progress:** To increase

capabilities and produce cutting-edge experiences, experiment with and invest in new technologies. Testing and prototyping can aid in determining viability and improving concepts.

**3. Give User Experience Priority:** Make user-centered design a top priority to make sure virtual environments are accessible, easy to use, and engaging. Produce interactive, immersive content that makes the most of the Metaverse.

**4. Address Privacy and Security Concerns:** Implement strong security measures and promote privacy best practices to protect user data and prevent cyber threats.

**5. Adapt to Regulatory and Ethical Challenges:** Stay compliant with regulations and address ethical considerations to foster a fair and inclusive Metaverse.

**6. Explore Economic Opportunities:** Innovate and explore new business models tailored to the Metaverse. Assess financial implications and develop strategies for sustainable growth.

**7. Foster a Culture of Innovation:** Encourage creativity and experimentation to drive innovation and stay ahead of the curve. Invest in research and development to explore new technologies and applications.

**8. Plan for Long-Term Sustainability:** Consider environmental impact and develop scalable solutions to ensure long-term relevance and success in the Metaverse.

- **Looking Ahead**

As the Metaverse continues to evolve, it will undoubtedly bring about significant changes and challenges. The ability to navigate this dynamic landscape will depend on adaptability, foresight, and a commitment to continuous improvement. By staying informed, embracing technological advancements, and addressing key challenges, individuals and organizations can position themselves for success in the Metaverse.

The journey ahead will require collaboration, creativity, and a shared vision for the future of digital spaces. As we move forward, the Metaverse has the potential to create new opportunities for connection, innovation, and growth, transforming how we interact with technology and each other. By preparing for what's next and embracing the possibilities of the Metaverse, we can shape a vibrant and impactful digital future.

In conclusion, the Metaverse represents an exciting and transformative evolution in digital interaction. By understanding its potential, addressing its challenges, and preparing for its future, we can navigate this new frontier and unlock the opportunities it offers. The journey into the Metaverse is just beginning, and its development will shape the future of technology and human connection in profound ways.

www.ingramcontent.com/pod-product-compliance
Lightning Source LLC
Chambersburg PA
CBHW071912210526
45479CB00002B/390